MW00337654

"My wife and I absolutely love Matt McMillen's book, *The Christian Identity*. It's been tremendous for our marriage and relationship with Jesus. Matt has definitely been blessed by God to share the Good News!" -*Amazon Customer*

"Matt brilliantly explains the supernatural transformation that happens when we become believers in the finished work of the cross. His writing style makes this easy to understand as he answers some of the toughest questions that are on so many Christians' minds today." -*Amazon Customer*

"This book is full of hope and grace. It explains that salvation can never be lost. It explains the goodness and mercy of our Father in heaven! It will fill you with a sense of joy and peace and give you relief from your burdens. Matt does a great job of explaining a lot of tough questions, and he lists verses from our Lord's Word to back up his thoughts on these subjects. Thanks Matt. What a blessing!" -*Amazon Customer*

Matt McMillen is a bestselling Christian author and teacher of God's Word. His books and massive social media ministry has taught countless amounts of people their true identity in Christ. Matt's easy-to-understand biblical teachings have helped build confidence in his readers, break lifelong addictions, and find their true purpose for living: enjoying God's grace through Jesus Christ!

For more information on his ministry, visit:
www.mattmcmillenministries.com

THE
CHRISTIAN IDENTITY

VOLUME 1

Discovering What Jesus Has Truly Done to Us

MATT MCMILLEN

Copyright © 2018 Matt McMillen
The Christian Identity, Volume 1
Discovering What Jesus Has Truly Done to Us

Published by: Matt McMillen Ministries
720 W. Karsch Blvd.
Farmington, MO 63640
matt@mattmcmillen.com

Printed in the United States of America

ISBN 978-0-9971533-4-7

For Jennifer. I love you more than I could possibly ever express in words. Thank you for being my wife.

Contents

*"But whoever is united with the Lord
is one with him in spirit."*
1 Corinthians 6:17

Introduction

Who Are You, Christian?

"Woof, woof, woof!" barks ring out.

"It's okay… It's okay… C'mere. I'm not going to hurt you."

"Grrrrrrrr…" a low growl starts to rumble as the man stoops down and moves closer. Reaching out he says, "I'm here to help. Don't be afraid"—but then gets bit. "Ow! My goodness, boy. Hold still."

Boy? Yes, a boy, but not a dog… a *human* boy.

Social services were called into an area of Siberia to investigate a child who was acting like a dog—a boy who had never been to school. This kid was walking around on all-fours, expressing aggressive behavior, and snarling rather than speaking.

But why? Why was this kid behaving like a dog? Because he thought he *was* a dog.

This is a true story.

Abandoned by both of his parents as a toddler, a dog raised him. Therefore, he was brought up to *think* he was something in which he was not. Sadly, this happens to *Christians* everywhere, all throughout the world. We are influenced to believe certain things about ourselves that simply are not true.

Because of inauthentic expressions around us, which come by way of Scripture being taken out of context, we act out fallacies in which God never intended for His children.

So, who are we? Those of us who've believed in Jesus Christ for His forgiveness, what is the truth about our identity? Are we sinful and wicked? Or are we holy and loving?

Do we have two selves—a good self and bad self? Or do we have one self, a *good* self, and a mind that's being renewed by the Holy Spirit each day?

Is God disappointed and angry at us? Or is He satisfied with the sacrifice of Jesus and our faith in that event? Where do we stand with our Creator? How close *are* we? How can we have confidence as a child of God? What is the biblical truth about our identity?

These are all legitimate questions that matter. They matter because the answers will either keep us in bondage or set us free—in our minds.

Many of us *have* been born into the family of God, we've received the identity He's given. Yet, we've been incorrectly influenced to think we need to sniff our food before we eat, scratch off fleas, and howl when other dogs are howling—but we don't.

Friend, we are not dogs. We can stand tall, speak clearly, and love others well. We are new creations in Christ. The Holy Spirit wants to teach us more and more about who we *really* are, every moment of our lives. He's not only with us, but He's in us. Even better, He's joined us for good!

I'm very happy you decided to read this book. Over the course of the next thirty days I hope I can help you learn more about the truth of your identity, Christian. My prayer is that you will grow in confidence in your true supernatural state. You might be pleasantly surprised at what God has done to your spirit! If you're *not* a Christian, don't let that stop you from reading this book. Maybe I can shine a light on some of the dark things you think about us. Things which are the behavior of "canines" and not Christians.

If you enjoy any of these devotionals to the point of wanting to share them with others, you can do so on my website: www.mattmcmillen.com. They're always available for free to share on social media, email to loved ones, or even print out to give away.

Take your time with this book. Don't skip ahead. Some things you're about to read will make "sniffing at the ground" seem strange. If you've got questions, check out the Bible passages I've used to back up what I've written, or you can even email me at matt@mattmcmillen.com.

But please, more than anything, read each day with an open mind and allow me to make the case for your *real* Christian identity! Believer, the word gospel means good news for a reason! What Jesus Christ has done *for* you, *to* you, and now *through* you, is really good news!

Day 1

The Greatest Spiritual Gift Is Love

"But the greatest of these is love."

See 1 Corinthians 13:13

G*randma.* This one word brings a feeling of peace to my soul. Just think-ing about her in adoration, as a man in his late 30's, I get a lump in my throat. I just *know* I wouldn't be who I am today without her.

To be clear, I don't want to put God in a box, because He can do whatever He wants. But I doubt I would have turned out like I am without Grandma raising me. Being brought up by the example of this angel-lady *has* to be why my fingers are typing this devotional, right now.

An understatement would be this: *my childhood was rough.* Mom and Dad couldn't get along, things got nasty, and all five of us kids were thrown into a hurricane of heartache. But in the eye of that storm was Grandma.

"Come here, baby. Let Grandma help you," was a familiar and comforting phrase I heard quite often as a child. This boisterous, amazing, fat little lady who could cook like no other, raised my brothers, sister, and me. Grandma knew we were in pain because of the divorce, constant moving and litigation, so she never added additional discomfort to us by being mean–ever. Even while correcting us she did so in such a loving way we couldn't ignore her or keep on acting out.

The love she expressed at all times, even in conflict, baffles me. Although I'm coming up on 38 years old, I've never met a person like her. I thought one day I would, but I haven't. Raising us in the 90's, when she should have been enjoying retirement, *still* has me in awe this very moment. She'll tell you though, "I wouldn't have had it any other way."

I can remember one time I got real bad sick, I'm talking *bad*. My agony was so great I couldn't even move. Laid up on the bottom bunk in my bedroom, Grandma came in every hour on the hour to sit on the side of the bed and rub my head with a cold, wet rag. I was so sick I couldn't always open my eyes, but I'd still feel her come in and hum sweet songs while wiping me down.

"There you go, baby. You should be good for a little while longer. Let Grandma know if I can do anything else for you, okay?"

She always called us *baby*, and at times we'd retort, "Grandma, why do you say that so much?"

"Well, because you're Grandma's babies."

In my teenage years I'd say, "I'm 15 years old. I'm not your baby."

"Oh hush your mouth, yes you are," then she'd wink at me and smile.

She wasn't the most talented person, she had no real hobbies, and Grandma wasn't super-smart. But I've *never* encountered anyone who expressed the gift of love like her. So many people want to say *this* gift and *that* gift is how you know the Spirit of Jesus lives in you. But love is the litmus test, and Grandma was in the Hall of Fame.

God has poured His love into the heart of every single believer–evenly. Grandma and I have the same amount of our Creator's love in us, and so do you, Christian. That *love* is the Spirit of Jesus Christ, Himself. How can I make such a claim? All we need to do is add up a handful of Bible verses and you'll see. First of all, God *is* love. Love is not just a characteristic of His but *who* He is. John writes those exact words:

> "... because God *is* love." (See 1 John 4:8)

Secondly, if God is love, we have love *in* us because we have the Spirit of Christ *in* us:

> "To them God has chosen to make known among the Gentiles the glorious riches of this mystery, *which is Christ in you*, the hope of glory." (Colossians 1:27)

So if God is love and Christ's Spirit–the Holy Spirit–is in us, then we *all* have a natural desire *to* love as new creations (see 2 Corinthians 5:17). It's simply up to us to *let* Jesus live through us, to produce love, just the same as a vine lives *through* a branch, to produce fruit (see John 15:5, Galatians 5:22,23).

Had I not experienced Grandma expressing the love of God–Jesus–who knows how I would have turned out. Mark, Luke, John, and Faith, all of us kids might be on a completely different path had she not planted seeds of love in our minds through her own actions and attitudes. She *showed* us how to let Jesus live *through* us.

Paul wrote to the Corinthians explaining what the love of God looks like:

> "Love is patient, love is kind. It does not envy, it does not boast, it is not proud. It does not dishonor others, it is not selfish, it is not easily angered, it keeps no record of wrongs. Love does not delight in evil but rejoices with the

truth. It always protects, always trusts, always hopes, always perseveres. Love never fails." (See 1 Corinthians 13:4-8)

For years I was under the impression that this is the type of love I have to strive for each day–but it's not. Paul is actually explaining God's love for *us*. Now, as we rest in His love we can exhale and then realize this same love has been programmed *in* to us as saints. The Ephesians are taught this truth:

"Grace be with all those who love our Lord Jesus Christ <u>with incorruptible love</u>." (Ephesians 6:24)

We *have* an incorruptible love inside of us. It is inextinguishable. It cannot change. I'm not talking about how we may feel at any given time, I'm talking about identity. Love, for a Christian, is organic. There's never a need to *force* our natural behaviors or thoughts. Instead, we are called to simply *be* our true selves as reborn children of God (see 1 John 3:1, John 1:12). What's already inside of us? Do that. Be that. Let it *out*.

Once I realized this "1 Corinthians 13 love" is our Creator's love for us through Christ, and *then* that Christ *lives* in us–the wheels started to pick up speed in my head. My mind was being renewed (see Romans 12:2, Philippians 1:6, 2:13).

"So all I need to do is wake up each day and be myself?" I asked God.

"Yes. And I'm going to teach you more and more about who you really are." His Holy Spirit spoke to *my* spirit, in a very motivating manner.

Grandma didn't "try" to love others each day, she simply allowed Christ to express Himself through her. He had given her the gift of love, and she too, gave that gift away. When I began to understand the New Covenant– that is, what Christ does *for* us, *to* us, and *through* us–this became apparent. She was just being herself at all times. The loving actions and attitudes were byproducts, supernatural fruit. All of that 1 Corinthians 13 stuff? All of that Galatians 5:22 and 23 fruit? My brothers, sister, and I got to enjoy! As did everyone Grandma encountered!

So today, my friends, know this: How simple is this gospel that God would choose to use us as His vessels? Extremely simple. Our unique personalities, interests, and gifts? God's desire is to show Himself to the world by way of them (see 2 Corinthians 5:20). We work together *with* Him, it's a relationship. The greatest gift of all time, love, is meant to impact this planet and ultimately eternity. Love is *in* you, Christian. Love is your identity. So allow Christ to use your loving identity, your gift, to walk out your true nature. Always be yourself, and always use your gift.

A prayer for you: *Heavenly Father, thank you for placing me in the lineage of my grandmother. By doing so, you blessed me before I was even born. I cannot express my gratitude in typed words, but you already know how I feel. Thank you, so much, for Grandma. Right now, I lift up all who are reading this, directly to you. I know that many of these dear readers never got to experience such a love from another person. For them, I'm asking you to reveal yourself in profound ways in their lives. You ARE love. The unconditional love Grandma showed me and others was YOUR SPIRIT through her—and I know that. Teach us more about the love you've poured out into every one of your children. Uncover the unloving parts of our thinking so we can let you live through us even more. Use us every moment to show off the greatest gift on planet earth, YOU. In Christ's name I pray, amen.*

Day 2

Why We Can Call God, Dad

*For you did not receive a spirit of slavery that
returns you to fear, but you received the Spirit
of sonship, by whom we cry, "Abba! Father!"*

Romans 8:15

Just imagine it, for a moment:

"Jennifer," I say abruptly to my wife as I walk into the kitchen. "I'm tired of doing housework, and I know you are too. All of this cooking and cleaning, to fix it, I think we should have another baby. We sure could use a servant around here."

"You know, I was just thinking the same thing," she replies intriguingly. "We definitely need a servant. We should bring in a new family member."

Now this sounds pretty stupid, doesn't it? Anyone in their right mind would say we were nuts, and the Division of Family Services would be called if this conversation actually got out. If this *really* happened, such a story would be at the top of everyone's newsfeed. Calling our kids *servants*, and then wanting more children just so *we* can be served? It's lunacy.

But many *Christians* believe this about *themselves* at times; thinking that God created us for duty, just to be "the help." The good news is, nothing could be further from the truth! God created us because He *loves* us, just like any caring parent would do! Yes, we must be forgiven and reborn through Christ, but once our sin issue has been dealt with once and for all time–by grace through faith in the Cross–we are His kids, and He is our Dad.

I don't want to be misunderstood here, kids *do* serve their parents, but not from a fear-filled obligation. When young children or teenagers are serving properly–or adult children–it's always out of love and respect. It's done with reverence and honor. Children are *not* servants, we are people. We have feelings. We have lives. We have hopes and dreams. Good parents understand this, and these things matter to them.

Like any good parent, God did not cause us to become His children to serve Him. On the contrary, once we become His child, we have the heart of a servant because Jesus is one with us. *He* is the greatest Servant of all time and *as* He lives through us we will serve God and others naturally.

When we feel forced to serve–guilted or obligated, condemned or "less than" if we don't–that's not coming from Christ within. It's coming from demonic forces, the power of sin, our old, unrenewed thoughts–or selfish people who are addicted to religion and don't understand the easiness of the gospel. Hierarchies and submission replace Jesus in the minds of many devout churchgoers and church leaders. Don't fall for their passive-aggressive manipulation. Stay focused on God's love for you.

If we look even deeper into this topic of serving, although we serve in different ways according to the gifts we've been given (and this isn't always at a church), God doesn't *need* anything from us. He's completely self-sufficient:

"And <u>he is not served by human hands</u>, as if he <u>needed</u> anything. Rather,
he himself gives everyone life and breath and everything else."
(Acts 17:25)

Do you see the order? It is God who serves *us* with life, breath, and everything else, because He *is* life, breath, and everything else. The evidence of this is Jesus Christ. Jesus was and *is* God Almighty–in the flesh! God became flesh to serve *us* through saving us from our sin! (See John 1:1, Colossians 1:15-20). There has never been a greater act of service than what Jesus did. Why? Because He was perfect. Matthew recorded this truth in Christ's own words:

"just as the Son of Man <u>did not come to be served</u>, but <u>to serve</u>, and to
<u>give his life</u> as a ransom for many." (Matthew 20:28)

A grace-confused person might yell at me, "Yeah right, Matt! The Bible says we are to serve others!"

Friend, I know that, and we *will*, instinctively, as we simply be ourselves. Organic service to God and people happens as we come to understand an amazing fact: We are God's kids, and He is our Dad.

"Nope! That's just disrespectful, Matt! We should be afraid of God and *never* call Him Dad! If anything, we are to call Him Father!"

What do you think a father is? A dad. And it's actually *biblical* to call Him Dad. Paul tells the Romans:

For you did not receive a spirit of slavery that returns you to fear, but you
received the Spirit of sonship, by whom we cry, "Abba! Father!"
(Romans 8:15)

First, why would he mention slavery? Why would he mention fear? Because that's how the people lived before Christ caused them to be adopted into the family of God by faith (see Proverbs 9:10). On this side of the Cross we have nothing to fear because fear has to do with punishment and Jesus was punished in full (see 1 John 2:2, 4:18, Romans 5:1, 2 Corinthians 5:21). Slavery and fear is not a father/child relationship, it's a master/servant relationship. It's a relationship of, "Do this or else!"

That's not the gospel.

Second, the word *Abba* means *Daddy*. A servant would never call their master *Daddy*. Daddy is a term of endearment. In the Middle East, *Abba* is what a child calls their father to this very day. When they say, "Daddy!" it's comforting. They know they are protected.

So, Abba means Daddy, and Daddy means *Dad*. You, Christian, can call the Creator of the universe, Dad–and He wants you to. In your mind, He wants you to cuddle up next to Him, pour out your concerns, and then trust Him. Your one-time faith in Jesus Christ gives you this right (see Hebrews 4:16, Ephesians 3:12). To be clear, your identity is *already* cuddled up to Him, you are *inside* of Him (see Colossians 3:3). But He wants your thought life to match up with this truth (see Romans 12:2, Philippians 4:8, Hebrews 3:1).

In Romans 8:15, Paul is teaching the church they don't need to be afraid of God, but to depend on God. He tells them they are no longer servants, but children.

If you think about it, why would we need to be afraid of God after we've placed our faith in the forgiveness of Jesus? It would only be because of our sins. However, Jesus has *removed* all of our sins *from* us at the Cross–past, present, and future–because He's not bound by time. Every single sin of ours was in the future when Christ died, so when we believed, they were removed (see John 1:29, Hebrews 9:22, 2 Peter 3:8).

Unlike the blood of the Old Covenant, animal blood, which only *covered* sins for a year at a time, Jesus has a much better method of dealing with sins. He removes them permanently from all who will believe in Him *one time* in history! (See Hebrews 7:22, 10:1,4,10,14, John 19:30, 1 John 3:5).

As children of God, Dad is *not* punishing us for our sin, and He never *will* punish us for our sin. Not a single one. Why not? Because every sin requires a bloody death–from jealousy to murder–and Jesus died *once*. He's not dying again and again in heaven for each sin we commit. He's resting just fine, never to die again! Therefore, He *purified* us once and for all time *from* sin–that is, our spirit. God is not dealing with us on the basis of our sins any longer, but on the basis of a loving father/child relationship (see Romans 6:23, Hebrews 1:3, 7:25, 10:10, John 1:12, Romans 8:15, Ephesians 1:5).

"I like this, Matt. It's making sense to me. Jesus' blood was enough to make my spirit brand new. So what should I do when I sin?"

Stop it. Turn from it. When it comes to sin–legalistic or licentious–never stop stopping. Never stop turning. Sin will never pay off. It will never fulfill you. You've been recreated to *not* sin. You don't even *want* to sin. This is why it always feels weird when you choose *to* sin. You are supernaturally holy, just the same as Jesus (see Romans 6:2, 2 Corinthians 5:17, Colossians 1:22, 1 John 4:17). But be sure to know, you don't stop sinning to stay saved, nor do you turn from sin to continue being God's child. Only Christ's life keeps your place in the family of God secure. *His* life, and nothing else.

This is vital to understand as a saint because Jesus is never going to die again–so neither are you! Your incorrect actions and attitudes–sins–will never cause Christ to perish! His life is much more powerful than any wrong choice we make, or sinful thought we have. Here's proof:

> *"Therefore <u>he is able to save completely</u> those who come to God through him, <u>because he always lives</u> to intercede for them." (Hebrews 7:25)*

"Because I live, you also will live." (See John 14:19)

Believer, *your* life–your salvation–is *Christ's* life! Repenting and confessing isn't–Jesus is! Yes, repenting and confessing of our immaturities is normal and healthy, but neither can keep us saved or make us more forgiven than we are right now. Only by death being defeated can we live and stay forgiven because every sin requires death! (See Romans 6:23). Jesus has won the battle *over* death, so you have too! Paul tells the people in Colossae:

"When <u>Christ who is your life</u> appears, then you also will appear with him in glory." (Colossians 3:4)

This is not later, but now! The only thing that will be different later–when He *physically* comes back–is we will get new physical bodies like He has. You know, the type of body He rose from the dead with? Poppin' in and out of thin air, ascending into the sky and stuff? (See 1 Corinthians 15:52).

When I came to understand this truth, that Jesus' eternal life is my eternal life, the most famous Bible verse of all time began to glow:

"For God so loved the world, that He gave His only begotten Son, that whoever believes in Him <u>shall not perish, but have eternal life</u>."
(John 3:16)

Who is it that has eternal life? A life with no beginning or end? JESUS! So, we receive *His* life as *our* life which causes us to always be in His family! Therefore, we can always call God, Dad, because we are coheirs with Christ! (See Romans 8:17).

Yet still, a behavior-focused person might say, "God is our King! We are to worship Him, bow down, and never dishonor Him by calling Him Dad!"

Friend, yes, He is King. But we are His royal children. We are on a different level than the rest of the world, than the unbelievers. We are children *of* the King. The King is our Dad, so we don't bow down in fear. We walk right up to Him and sit on His lap *on* the throne–fearless, full of trust, admiration, comfort, security, and love. The Cross has made this relationship possible, because the Cross has removed our sins. That event, and our faith in it, birthed us into regal, celestial immortally.

And yes, we worship Him, but not out of obligation or anxiety. Instead, out of gratitude. Out of thankfulness. Out of the sense of stability in which He freely gives us as Abba. There's no need to worship God "Because me must!" "Because He needs it!" or because of fear. Remember, fear has to do with punishment and Jesus was already punished plenty. Our Dad's love for us is perfect (see Romans 5:1, 1 John 4:18).

We are not serving God out of fear, nor worshiping Him to butter Him up or appease His ego. We are family and friends. We are no longer called servants. Read what Jesus said:

> *"I no longer call you servants, because a servant does not know his master's business. Instead, I have called you friends, for everything that I learned from my Father I have made known to you." (John 15:15)*

God has chosen to let all of us know His business. His business was formerly a mystery until Christ came. Now, through Jesus, the mystery of God is over. The mystery is the Spirit of Jesus Christ *in* us, permanently, by grace through faith, which has caused us to become children of God! (See Colossians 1:26-28, Hebrews 1:1-3, Ephesians 2:8,9, John 1:12).

So today, my friends, know this: The apostle John wrote his letter 1 John as an old man. It is said that as he was carried into the church of young believers, addressed in this letter, he always smiled at the crowd while repeating, "Love one another. Love one another. Love one another." This was John's message. The self-proclaimed, "Apostle whom Jesus loved" (see John 13:23) knew God loved us, and that God lives *in* us, causing *us* to love too. John also knew we had nothing to fear as His children. So excited about this truth, he penned, *"See what great love the Father has lavished on us, that we should be called children of God! And that is what we are!"* (See 1 John 3:1).

A prayer for you: *Dad, I love you. When I think about how big and strong you are, and that you're MY Dad, I get a lump in my throat and misty-eyed. I feel so protected. I feel so secure. You are my King, my Dad, my God, my everything. Thank you for making me your son. Right now, I lift up all who are reading this, directly to you. So many of them are unnecessarily afraid of you, they don't understand your perfect fatherly love. Today, I ask that you set them free from this fear. Your desire is to make them feel joyful, confident, and always full of hope! You never say, "Prove you are my child by worshiping me!" No. You say, "I love you just as you are. You are my masterpiece." Help them to grow in this loving relationship in which they have with you through Jesus. Help them to understand you aren't always serious, but sometimes funny, and sometimes playful. Help these dear readers to know that you enjoy life! And that you came to give us the most abundant life of all–life through Christ! Thank you for being our Dad. Amen.*

Day 3

Christians Are Not Sinners

*"But now he has reconciled you by Christ's physical
body through death to present you holy in his sight,
without blemish and free from accusation"*

Colossians 1:22

"I'm a sinner saved by grace!" This is a very popular thing to say, although not true. A more accurate statement for a Christian would be, "I *was* a sinner saved by grace! Now I'm a righteous, blameless, holy child of God!"

Here's another incorrect declaration to apply to a believer: "Hate the sin, love the sinner!"

Why is this inaccurate? Because Christians are not sinners, at all. Sure, we might have sinful actions and attitudes, but our identity is exactly like God's. We are a people of His very own nature. Peter tells the early church this same truth–who they actually are. Which, like today's church, was extremely hard to believe:

*"Through these he <u>has given us</u> his very great and precious promises,
so that through them you may <u>participate in the divine nature</u>, having
escaped the corruption in the world caused by evil desires." (2 Peter 1:4)*

Let's not skim over this verse. Both parts I've underlined can easily be ignored but are vital to understating our identity as Christians.

1. **has given us** — This is past tense. I repeat, this is *past tense*. This has already happened for every single believer in Christ. It's not happening, but it's finished. What's happened?
2. **participate in the divine nature** — We have been given God's very own nature! Christian, your *nature* has changed! It's not changing little by little, but you—right now—have a brand new heavenly nature!

Nature means natural. As in, no effort to *be*, no effort to *express*. Divine means heavenly! Divine means *like God*! So no matter what we do or don't do, our nature is the exact same as God's! (To know more about your nature, see 1 Corinthians 13:4-8, Galatians 5:22,23, 2 Peter 1:5-9, Philippians 4:8). It is *from* this nature our actions and attitudes become more and more organic! Our *do* begins to match up with our *who*, once we *know* who we are!

How is this possible? How can *we* have the same nature as the Creator of the universe–as Christ Himself? (See Colossians 1:16, Hebrews 1:2). Because we've been born again in our spirit. God's very own supernatural sperm–for lack of a better word–has been implanted in us to *give* us a new spiritual body. This happens the millisecond we believe Jesus has forgiven us. Whether we felt it or not, that doesn't matter. Our supernatural birth is not based on a feeling, but on a fact of faith (see 1 John 5:13, 2 Corinthians 13:5,6). If you felt something, great! God isn't against feelings, but those feelings did not save you. So if you *didn't* feel anything, don't worry, Christian, you *are* born again. This is why Jesus said:

> *"Flesh gives birth to flesh, but the Spirit gives birth to spirit. You should not be surprised at my saying, 'You must be born again.'"* (John 3:6,7)

The wonderful news of the gospel is we can't undo this birth! Just the same as we can't undo our earthly father's action of implanting his sperm into our mom–which created our unchangeable *physical* body–we can't undo receiving God's seed either, which recreated our unchangeable *spiritual* body! Our physical body inherited our parents' features and our spiritual body inherited God's! His divine sperm is forever infused *in* us which means we have His perfect nature! Physical DNA is permanent after birth, and spiritual DNA is permanent after *re*birth. As an old man, John explains:

> *"No one born of God makes a practice of sinning, for God's seed abides in him; and he cannot keep on sinning, because he <u>has been born of God</u>."*
> (1 John 3:9)

A lot of grace-confused Christians will use this verse as a threat, but that's not the point. The point is we don't even have the ability to continue sinning *in our spirit*. Our spirit, the real us, has been reborn and infused with God's own Spirit. We are literally sealed up *in Him* forever! (See John 3:6,7, 2 Corinthians 5:17, Romans 6:6,7, 1 John 3:1, Ephesians 1:13, Colossians 3:3).

This verse *describes* a Christian, it doesn't *prescribe* one. Sinning no longer makes sense to us in our nature. That's John's point. The entire book of 1 John is the description of the contrast between sinner and saint, believer and unbeliever, Gnostic and non-Gnostic, child of God and child of wrath–darkness and light. It's not how-to manual, but an explanation *of.*

So *when* we sin–not if–we are *not* being our true self. We are not express-ing Christ, our holiness. We are dogs meowing, cats barking, and roosters sleeping in. Sin makes no sense to us, but it does not *change* us. Our nature is final by birth.

I understand this is hard to fathom because of so much behavior-focused teaching out there. But if we can begin to refocus on *identity* as the church, our behavior will start to look a whole lot better and be a lot more natural.

Like the Pharisees who were fixated on behavior and not identity, we too can magnify how many times a person messes up, and how often, so *we* can judge who they "truly" are. Sadly, Jesus called these types of people "white-washed tombs–pretty on the outside, but dead bones within" (see Matthew 23:27). For us, holy children of God, the *opposite* can be said. We will always be beautiful on the inside, it's the outside we can incorrectly allow to become nasty. Whether with legalism or alcoholism, you name it, anything unholy coming *from* us is not natural *to* us.

Thankfully, God has rigged it this way for all who have believed in Jesus' ability to save them *once* (see Hebrews 10:10, 7:25). Being behavior-centered rather than identity-centered is not how the New Covenant works. On this side of the Cross, our only ministry for the *entire* world is that of complete rec-onciliation with God through Christ (see 2 Corinthians 5:18). So when we say, "Look at my awesome spiritual disciplines, just be like me!" we've veered off into the woods.

The New Covenant message is not "Stop sinning or else!" That was John the Baptist's and the teachers of the Law. John even said such legalism must go *away* in order to make room for Christ (see John 3:30).

The problem is, our unrenewed, behavior-addicted thinking wants to tell people, "Try harder!" "Commit to change!" "Do more!" But when we simply *live out* our divine nature, none of that pressure is necessary. Natural behavior is never forced. Natural behavior is never threatened or guilted into *being*. It just happens...naturally. This is why we need to start telling Christians who they *are*, not what to do. Only then will their *doing* sprout the sweetest fruit (see Galatians 5:22,23, John 15:5).

"But Matt, I still sin!"

Me too. Me too, friend. We all do, and we hate it. But we shouldn't hate *ourselves*–that's what Satan wants from us. Sinning never feels good permanently. It never makes long-term sense to us. It's a mirage set up by demonic forces and old thought patterns.

If you look even deeper into this you'll see that *disdain* for our unnatural behaviors–choosing to sin–is proof of our salvation. If we absolutely, *positively* don't care about our mistakes *then* we should worry about our saving. Yet still, in the same breath, some Christians go nearly their entire lifetime denying their divine nature. But when *they* are faithless *God* remains faithful for He cannot deny His own seed within them (see 2 Timothy 2:13, John 1:12).

Once we receive His supernatural sperm, by faith in Christ's forgiveness, it cannot be undone. We've inherited holiness. Inheritances cannot be reversed by the behavior of the beneficiary, nor worked for to achieve, sustain, or maintain. Inheritances come only by a death, and Christ died. Therefore, the promise to the Father by Christ at the Cross, and vice versa, sealed our fate as His holy children who were passed down an unearnable reward: *equal righteousness with Jesus Christ* (see John 19:30, Hebrews 6:16-19, 7:22, 25, 10:10, Ephesians 1:18, Romans 8:17, 2 Corinthians 5:20).

We are not sinners. We are not a *mixture* of sinner and saint. God is not sharing your spirit with anything that has to do with sin. Your spirit isn't being born again each time you mess up and then "get back on track." Nor does confessing cleanse you–you *are* cleansed. Confessing–which is simply agreeing with God–is normal and healthy. Repenting of sin is too. But neither confession nor repentance can improve who you already are. Instead, both knock off the hinderances keeping you from *enjoying* who you are (see 1 Corinthians 6:11, Hebrews 12:1-3, 2 Peter 1:5-9).

The truth is we have everything we need, today, this moment, for life and godliness! We've been blessed with every spiritual blessing! Jesus' very own Spirit! (See 2 Peter 1:3, Ephesians 1:3). We are children of God who sometimes forget who we are, therefore we express sin. We are learning and growing *from* our righteous identity, not to *keep* our righteous identity. Our supernatural DNA structure is final! It's unchangeable and secure!

"Nope! Matt, you're just giving people a license to sin!"

Friend, we don't need a license. We're all sinning just fine without one–Christians included. Further, God does not grade us on a curve based on how much or how little we sin. We *must* be perfect like *He* is perfect and the only way this can happen is if we are born into His very own family, once, by grace through faith (see Matthew 5:48, John 1:12, 3:16, Ephesians 2:8,9). The fact of the matter is *we* cannot sustain our supernatural birth by making different choices, just the same as *we* cannot sustain our *physical* birth by making different choices. We are born! Birth cannot be undone because of unnatural behaviors and mindsets!

"No way, Matt! I'm not buying it! We need to be tougher on sin! This stuff you're saying will cause people to go *crazy* in sin! Paul even said that *he* is the chief of sinners!"

I know at first glance this might come across as heresy. But I've never met a single person who finally understood their spiritual perfection and then used it to continue in legalism or to live licentiously. Never. The opposite happens.

The Jews who wanted to stay focused on legislating right and wrong behavior–rather than grace through faith in Jesus–they wanted to kill Paul for preaching this same thing I'm preaching (see Acts 26:21). Like many of our modern Christian teachers, these people thought grace would cause people to fall off the deep end, right into a chasm of doing bad stuff. However, Paul told Titus it is *grace* that teaches us *how* to live godly lives!

For the grace of God has appeared that offers salvation to all people. It teaches us to say "No" to ungodliness and worldly passions, and to live self-controlled, upright and godly lives in this present age (Titus 2:11,12)

Grace is our teacher, not our excuse. Grace keeps us centered on our identity because it's how we got saved in the first place.

Paul addresses the Corinthians as sanctified people–saints, holy ones– even though they were some of the worst-behaved Christians on the planet (see 1 Corinthians 1:2). Not once did he say their sinful actions and attitudes would cause God to go back on His New Covenant. Paul never said, "Stop taking advantage of God's grace! You might just wear it out with all that nasty sinnin'!"

No. Not once. Instead, he kept telling them who they still *are* even when they weren't living in their natural *way*. He said they've been remade to *not* sin, so *don't* sin. He lets them know they *have been* cleansed, so *live* cleansed (see 1 Corinthians 6:11). He even informs the Roman Christians–who were just about on par with the confused party-people in Corinth–that *when* they sin, God's grace increases, not decreases (See Romans 5:20). Such a verse reminds me of lyrics from the David Crowder song, *How He Loves:*

"If His grace is an ocean, we're all sinking."

And yes, Paul called himself the chief of sinners, but he was referencing his former life as a persecutor of the church. He's explaining to Timothy that his pointless life as a devout legalist was nothing more than dung. He's using his *former self* as an example of what God will do for the worst of people if they'll receive His Spirit into their's. He's not talking about his current identity in Christ. Just look at the context of the passage and you'll see how he references his past:

"Even though <u>I was once</u> a blasphemer and a persecutor and a violent man, <u>I was shown mercy</u> because I acted in ignorance and <u>unbelief</u>. The grace of our Lord <u>was poured out</u> on me abundantly, along with the faith and love that are in Christ Jesus. Here is a trustworthy saying that deserves full acceptance: Christ Jesus came into the world to save sinners—of whom I am the worst. But for that very reason <u>I was shown mercy</u> so that in me, the worst of sinners, Christ Jesus might display his immense patience <u>as an example</u> for those who <u>would believe in him and receive</u> eternal life." (1 Timothy 1:13-16)

Do you see it? Just like in Romans 7, Paul is referencing his past unbelieving self as an example of what *not* to do and how *not* to be like. After all, this is the very same apostle who tells us we *have been* reconciled with God through Christ; the same apostle who said the old *has gone* and the new *is here*; the same person who said his old self died and he got a new self! This is the same writer who penned we are holy, justified, *not* condemned, blameless, new creations, children of God, saints, seated in heavenly places—he said we have the mind of Christ, we are free from the Law, and we are infused with God's own Spirit forever! (See Romans 5:1, 6:6,7, 8:1,2, 10:4, 1 Corinthians 2:16, 6:17,19, 2 Corinthians 5:17,21, Colossians 1:22, 3:3, Galatians 2:20, 5:1, Ephesians 2:6).

So today, my friends, know this: Tell the truth about yourself *to* yourself. Sinner or saint, you will live out who you believe you are. If you think about it, if you *weren't* all these good things, then when you *do* good things, you're being a phony–a fake. If you're truly a sinner then what better an excuse to sin and not do good? I mean, why not? If sinning just comes natural then why deny yourself, and why would God recreate us as His children to live such a cruel, unnatural life? ... But, if you're *truly* a saint, then what better a reason to *be* yourself–to live it out?! Christian, you *are* a saint–so live!

A prayer for you: *Heavenly Father, thank you for teaching me who I am. It feels wonderful. In Romans 3, Paul lets us know about all of humanity's problem BEFORE we come to faith in Christ alone—which is falling short of your glory. But now, as saints, this verse does not apply to us because we HAVE your glory! Jesus even said so in John 17:22! It's Him IN us! Paul said the same thing in 2 Corinthians 3:18! Thank you so much for this free gift of glory! And Dad, the mistranslation of the word "flesh" into "sinful nature" in the NIV Bible has misinformed so many people about their identity. The original word was "sarx" which means "flesh." We don't have a sinful nature, we have flesh that can be used in a sinful way if we incorrectly choose to do so. But even our flesh is not sinful—it was your idea! The Gnostics who were talked about in 1 John thought flesh was bad—but it's not! We have YOUR nature, even in these bodies! We are not feeding a good dog and a bad dog inside of us, we are simply being ourselves when we live holy lives! We don't have a bad dog! Sure, we have unrenewed thinking and old bad habits, but you are helping us with those each day—and you'll never leave us. We are grateful. Right now, I lift up all who are reading this, directly to you. Teach them who they are, Father. Teach them that if they've placed their faith in Jesus, one time, 1 John 4:17 says they're exactly like Him, today. Hebrews 10:14 says they've been made perfect forever! And if they haven't yet believed, let them know they can become a saint and no longer a sinner, by simply believing Jesus has forgiven them. In His powerful name I pray, amen.*

Day 4

The Danger of Mixing the Old
and New Covenants

"No one pours new wine into old wineskins.
Otherwise, the wine will burst the skins, and both
the wine and the wineskins will be ruined. No,
they pour new wine into new wineskins." ~Jesus

Mark 2:22

"Matt, you're just confusing people! Stick to the Bible and teach God's Word!" a furious comment shows up under my post.

"Maybe try decaf?" I say in my mind but don't type, after receiving yet again, hate-filled attacks from supposedly another Christian. They forgot about that love one another thing Jesus commanded.

Almost instantly the enemy presses me to use my gift of word compilation to fire away, pointing out their hypocrisy according to the Law and "setting them straight" with the truth of the New Covenant. But I'm not falling for it.

This isn't my first go-round with a Mosaic Law-abiding citizen, or even this specific person. Plus, I used to mix in Moses' commandments with Jesus' too, so I know their M.O.

For years, rather than allow the Spirit to lead me, I made the mistake of using 613 Old Testament commandments as a buffet line just like they're doing. So I can empathize with their bondage.

Sadly, this person sits on the sideline of Facebook and waits for me to write about the differences in the Old and New Covenants. Like a streaker, they'll run onto the field of my post, attempting to get attention from the crowd without making any biblical sense. Innocently, I'll give them that.

"If it's in the Bible, it applies to me! If it's in red letters, we're *all* supposed to do it!"

Such words have ruined many lives. From the angry pulpits, overbearing relatives, and friends who've found religion, opening up the Bible randomly and applying the words to our lives and others can cause carnage—*if* we aren't separating the Covenants. We're missing the point of Jesus Christ's entire life when we combine the Old Covenant with the New Covenant.

Christ came to teach the full extent of the Old Covenant—the Law—not to abolish it but reveal the true standard to the self-righteous people who believed they were actually living by it (see Matthew 5:17). This is why some of the red letters can be very deadly. They were supposed to be (see 2 Corinthians 3:6). When Jesus taught Law He was setting people up for failure so that they'd lean toward faith in Him alone.

Jesus never mixed the two Covenants, but instead, explained the paradoxes. Who are we to say He was exaggerating as He gave very difficult—no, impossible—behavior passages? Not once did He say, "Give it your best shot and God will grade you on a curve," never. He said, "You must be absolutely perfect like God if you want to live by the Law. Here's the standard. Don't you *dare* disregard a single commandment or you'll be least in the kingdom and in danger of hell" (see Matthew 5 & 6).

Combining the two Covenants creates double-talk and confusion in the fullest. This is why Jesus wanted to be perfectly clear about living by the Law: "Don't even dip your toe in it. If you fail at one of the 613–ten of which were the Ten Commandments–you fail at all of them. Not one jot or tittle can be set aside by you. As much as it hurts your pride, you must give up on Law completely, and instead, believe in me *only*" (see Matthew 5:19, 11:28-30, John 1:12).

The good news is, if combining the two creates bondage, separating them sets us free! (See John 8:32).

Because our world is changing so much, in regard to reaching others and how we do it, I've been very active with my ministry on social media for years. Online aggression is nothing new, from both the believer and the non-believer. Most of the time I overlook it and move on, but on occasion I'll spend a while attempting to explain that not all of the words in the Bible were written to Christians.

Now, *should* all Christians know the words in the Bible, even the stuff not written to us? Of course. From front to back the Bible is true. But we must keep everything in context. We must decode whether or not the Old or New Covenant is being referenced in each verse, passage, section, and book. Especially when Jesus was speaking.

Satan wants us to try to do stuff, and not do stuff, that God never intended for us. The devil and his demons love turmoil and conflict, both with other people and in our minds.

There's a dividing line in the Bible when we Christians came into play. It's not the page *before* the book of Matthew, which reads, *The New Testament*. It is the Cross. It's not the *birth* of Jesus but the *death* of Jesus because only blood can bring in a New Covenant (see Hebrews 7:22, 8:6, 9:18). When

His blood was shed He opened up the opportunity for the entire world to be saved through faith in Him (see Colossians 1:26,27). Before this happened we non-Jews were without hope. Paul tells the Gentile Christians in Ephesus:

> *"remember that at that time you were separate from Christ, excluded*
> *from citizenship in Israel and foreigners to the covenants of the promise,*
> *without hope and without God in the world." (Ephesians 2:12)*

Israel was not a geographical location until 1948. This verse is about the Jewish *people,* not the country. So we must face a truth that's hard to swallow, especially when we've been taught to obey the Law given to Israel: *Jesus' ministry before the Cross was for the Jews only.*

The ability to be a Christian had not yet happened for the Gentiles–all of the non-Jews on planet earth. God had made a Covenant with Israel, not us (see Exodus 24:8, 34:27, Galatians 4:4,5).

The title of "Christian" did not exist until after Jesus came back to life. Before His resurrection, Jew *or* Gentile were the only options. Christ came to preach to the Jews–also called Israel–because they were part of the Covenant given by God through Moses. After the Cross–after blood was shed to bring in the New Covenant–there is neither Jew nor Gentile. We all become one in Christ, a new creation all together! (See Hebrews 1:3, 7:22, 10:10,14,26-29, Galatians 3:28, 2 Corinthians 5:17).

Because the New Covenant had not yet been established–and because God can only work through one Covenant at a time (see Hebrews 8:6,13, 10:9,16)–unless we were part of the group of people led through the Red Sea floor, Jesus was not speaking to us *in* the gospels. He came to minister to the Jews *only* before He had died. Yes, we can look back and glean, and we should, but this is not our mail.

The authors of the gospels wrote what they did so both the Jew and the Gentile would see Christ as the Son of God and believe. But the content in all four books was for the Jewish race according to the Old Covenant.

Case in point, in Matthew 15:21-28, there's an account of a Canaanite woman begging Jesus to heal her daughter. Jesus ignores her, but she keeps asking. Why did He blow her off? She was Canaanite, not Jewish. The disciples urged Him to tell her to buzz off, eventually He turned and said, "I was only sent to the lost sheep of Israel."

Who were the lost sheep of Israel? The Jews who weren't believing in God by faith, but attempting to achieve righteousness by the Law (see Galatians 3:11). They had replaced their relationship with Yahweh, with religion. Israel were those who Moses led out of slavery in Egypt, those who were *given* the Law, *by* Moses, at the base of Mount Sinai. The people of Canaan were not there. God did not establish His Covenant with this woman's heathen ancestors, so Jesus kept walking.

So, why would they be *lost* if they were *already* God's chosen people? It's the same reason *we* can be lost on *this* side of the Cross: unbelief in Christ alone and self-righteousness through Mosaic legalism.

However, there's something very special that happens in the story of the Canaanite woman, a foreshadowing of Christ allowing a non-Jew to be helped by Him through faith. While being called a *dog* because she was a Gentile, she continues to beg Jesus for help. "I'll take the crumbs from the table!"

In essence, the Canaanite lady was pleading, "I know I'm not Jewish, but I still believe in your ability to heal my child!"

Moved by her faith in Him, Christ heals her daughter.

This goes to show that God has always dealt with humanity by faith, even before the Law. The Law is thousands of years old, God's relationship with mankind is much older. This is why the New Covenant is older than the Old Covenant. "Do you believe me?" has always been God's litmus test for fellowship.

But Jesus still had to deal with the racism and bigotry of the House of Israel, of His own fleshly lineage. For this reason, Christ was born under the Law to redeem the people *under the Law* (see Galatians 4:4). You and I, we were never given the Law, so observing it is ridiculous. We would be laughed at if we *attempted* to obey a single commandment.

Therefore, as New Covenant people who try to mix the Old in with the New–even a drop–such is a dangerous concoction. Moses plus Jesus doesn't work, and here's why:

> *"For the Law was given through Moses; grace and truth came through Jesus Christ." (John 1:17)*

Do we want Law (you can only choose this if you're Jewish)? Or do we want grace and truth (the only option for the Gentile)? We can't have both. Jesus explains:

> *"No one pours new wine into old wineskins. Otherwise, the wine will burst the skins, and both the wine and the wineskins will be ruined. No, they pour new wine into new wineskins." (Mark 2:22)*

Christian, you are new–that is, your spirit. The Covenant is new as well. This is why compatibility with God *after* the Cross is possible. The Law is the Old Covenant. Grace and truth is the New Covenant! New wine is the New Covenant, old wineskins is the Old!

I don't want to be misunderstood, I'm *not* saying the Law is wrong or flawed in any way. I'm saying it's perfect (see Romans 7:12). But if righteousness could come by the Law there wouldn't be a need for anything new; the Law was a tutor until the Teacher had come (see Galatians 2:21, 3:24, John 14:26). Because of its perfect standards and our inability to live by such–the

Jews, of course, not us–humanity had to have another way. For this reason Jesus said:

> "*I am the way and the truth and the life. No one comes to the Father except through me.*" (*John 14:6*)

The person who was attacking me on social media had been taught to mix the Old and the New from the time they were little. They told me so. What was happening as a result? The wineskins bursting. Anger, resentment, legalistic bitterness, comparison of their ability to keep *parts* of the Law to both me and others.

Then they dropped the bomb, "I'm in my 60's so I know what the truth is!"

I wanted to say, "Just because something is old doesn't mean it's true," but I kept an even keel and didn't disrespect them.

Old does not mean correct. The early church "fathers"–heavy on quotations because we are to call no man *father* (see Matthew 23:9)–they branched off into divisions from the beginning. Faith in Christ alone wasn't enough. Those who struggled with self-righteousness needed their ears tickled so they added Moses back in, as well as creating "hierarchies of holiness" and brand new church laws (see Galatians chapters 1 through 5, Revelation 2:4).

What makes something *true* is if it's biblical and the interpretation is correct based on context. Not if it's old. Islam is old too. Satanic worship is even older.

I gave my best shot at explaining this with gentleness and respect, they didn't care though. They continued to belittle me while being extremely passive-aggressive in order to appear in control. This person remained severely condescending toward me about rightly dividing God's Word into Old and New Covenant. Just the same as the devout Jewish people did toward Christ's good news, I was "twisting the Scriptures."

In nearly everything Jesus taught He was comparing the Old and New Covenants. He was comparing slavery and freedom, heavy and light burdens, work and rest, death and life, wide roads of Law and narrow gates of grace. According to the Old Covenant, you worked *really* hard, attempting to obey 613 commandments to achieve righteousness with God (see Deuteronomy 6:25). The Jews were instructed to mediate on the Law day and night (Psalm 1:2). They were taught they'd be successful, rich, and prosperous by obeying *all* of the commandments (see Joshua 1:8). This is why wealthy and healthy people bragged on their righteousness.

According to the New, we are to simply rest in faith in *Christ's* finished work (see Matthew 11:28-30, John 15:4,5, 19:30, Hebrews 4:11, 10:12, Ephesians 2:8,9, Romans 6:14). We're taught it's easier for a camel to fit through the eye of a needle, than for someone who's become rich through Law observance to make it to heaven. This blew the disciples' minds! (See Matthew 16:26, 19:24, Luke 18:18-27). Jesus flipped the tables of the Jews both literally and spiritually! (See Matthew 21:12, John 5:39,40).

The most well-behaved, outwardly-righteous people on the planet had to repent! Repent of what? Unbelief in Jesus Christ! (Matthew 23:27,28, Hebrews 10:26-30). Even for the life-long, scripturally-seasoned, educated scholar, they had to change their belief! New Covenant teaching grabs a person's ego, slaps it on the back of the neck and says, "Get outta here! You're not needed! In Christ we *have* everything!" (See Philippians 3:1-9).

Understanding the life of Christ–that His ministry was about the difference in the Old and New Covenants–is paramount in knowing who we truly are as New Covenant believers. Let's look at a few examples from the gospels to see what I mean:

1. **Martha and Mary.** In Luke 10:38-42, there's a story of Jesus visiting the home of two sisters. While He was there, Mary sat at His

feet *resting* and Martha was going bonkers trying to prepare stuff *for* Him—but He was already there. Jesus kindly corrected Martha and said Mary had chosen wisely. Martha is the Old Covenant, Mary is the New Covenant.

2. **The Parable of the Prodigal Son.** This famous account is found in Luke 15:15-32. It's heavily used by people who struggle with legalism as a story of behavior repentance in order to be accepted by God. But the Holy Spirit has revealed to me an even deeper way of seeing this parable. The son who leaves home is us Gentiles, and the son who stayed home is the Jews. When we Gentiles came home to God through faith—not by cleaning up our act—the Father embraced us without *us* saying a word. Even though the son had a speech all planned out, the Father didn't want to hear it. Instead, He hugged him with all His might and threw a party. This caused the son to remember who he was and what family he was born into. This is the New Covenant. The Jews, however, were the *older* brother in the story. Salty because the Father accepted the "bad son" with no questions asked, the older brother stayed *outside* of the party *fuming* because he was so well-behaved for so long. The older brother is the Old Covenant, and as you can see, the Old has no place in the Father's House Party. So who was the true prodigal in the end? The Old.

3. **The Parable of the Talents, and the Parable of the Vineyard Workers** (see Matthew 20:1-16, 25:14-30). Two different parables, two different ways of God's judgment. One judgment according to the Old Covenant, and the other judgment according to the New Covenant. What happens in the Old? The people are judged by their performance and get rewarded based on such. What happens in the New? They all get paid the same in the end, no matter what time of day they began.

Friend, Jesus taught the Old Covenant in its purest form to shut up the mouths of the sanctimonious—not to stroke their egos (see Matthew 5:17,18, Romans 3:19). The Law is meant to do the same for people today. He didn't come to abolish it but to unroll it all the way out and say, "Go ahead. Try. Be perfect like God is perfect—or take a hike" (see Matthew 5:48).

This flies in the face of Christians who struggle with Mosaic legalism, which is an oxymoron because we were never even *given* the set of 613 commandments to begin with. Do a quick Google search of "What are the 613 commandments in the Law" and you'll be bored to tears before you finish reading half of them. Remember, you must keep *all* of them if you want to live by them (see Deuteronomy 4:2, Galatians 3:10).

Yet we want to cherry-pick the Ten Commandments—or "the Nine"—because nobody keeps the real Sabbath, which was from Friday to Saturday. Then we want to denigrate the Law even *more* by sprinkling in tithing so that we can be entered into the church lotto every Sunday morning. This is *really* sad, because the only time Jesus mentions the tithe is when He was ripping into the unbelievers due to their laughable Law-following (see Matthew 23:23). Yet we want to tell people God will bless them because they pay money? It's lunacy.

Rebuking the devour by giving ten percent of your food to the unemployed priests—not cash—was part of the Law. Who's Law? Israel's. Not ours. Oh, it's convenient for the people teaching this fallacy, but it's not the gospel. Extorting believers is a sin. Why not just let your needs be known and allow people give freely because they're excited about the message? We *give* in the same manner in which we received our salvation—by grace. We've *already* been blessed with every spiritual blessing! (See Ephesians 1:3). There's not a single verse in any New Testament letter that commands a Christian to give an exact percentage of their money away. Instead, we are to give freely, from the heart, *not* under pressure (see 2 Corinthians 9:7).

Do you see the danger of mixing the two Covenants? Aggressive people. Guilt. Condemnation. Quasi-grace. Give to get. Double-talk. "Yeah, you're forgiven, but not really." Pressure-filled, "Be like me!" teaching. And *then* Christians who experience such will struggle with crippling fear and anxiety, sometimes resulting in suicidal thoughts, *"Why am I not good enough?"*

Then they'll punish *themselves*, attempting to relieve the pain. Some don't *kill* themselves, but they'll cut their bodies and confidence, "Because I deserve it," they'll say.

This same hazardous concoction of mixing Old and New is what got Jesus killed. The Jews could *not* separate the two and it ticked them off to the point of plotting against Jesus, spitting in His face, beating Him to a bloody pulp, then brutally murdering Him. That's what Law does. It is a ministry of *death* and death is what you'll get when you place someone under it (see 2 Corinthians 3:7-18).

This is why, in our minds, the Old must be gone completely *so that* we can enjoy the New! (See Galatians 2:19, Romans 7:4). The Law hasn't died but we've said, "Uncle!" and repented of trying to obey a single command! We've turned *away* from Law and *toward* faith in Christ alone! We've stopped trusting Jesus for *only* His saving blood, but now for the guidance of His Spirit too!

Jesus' New Covenant only has *two* commandments: believe and love (see John 13:34,35, 1 John 3:23).

I can already hear a Law-lover screaming at me, "You're so wrong, Matt! Jesus said we are to love God with all of our heart, soul, and mind! And to love our neighbor as ourself!"

…Friend, yes, He did, but that is love *according to the Law*. Anytime Jesus was asked a Law-based question He gave a Law-based answer. Just look:

"Teacher, which is the greatest commandment <u>in the Law</u>?"

Jesus replied: "'Love the Lord your God with all your heart and with all your soul and with all your mind.' This is the first and greatest commandment. And the second is like it: 'Love your neighbor as yourself.' All the Law and the Prophets hang on these two commandments." (Matthew 22:36-40)

Do you see it? So many of us allow our heads to explode when we see the word *commandment*. We immediately mix Moses' 613 in with Jesus' two. If we aren't deciphering the commandments of the Old and New Covenants, we mix them together, therefore causing a sulfurous combustion. Jesus' commandments are not burdensome (1 John 5:3). Moses' were (Deuteronomy 4:2, James 2:10, Galatians 3:10). The Old Covenant was about stressing out while trying and *trying* to love God with everything we are! The New Covenant is about relaxing and realizing God has loved *us* with everything *He* is, through His Son (see John 3:16, Romans 5:8).

So today, my friends, know this: As a person who has believed in Christ's forgiveness, once, you are the beneficiary to the Covenant between the Father and the Son, established by blood at the Cross. You've been taken *out* of the equation, set aside, and now you simply benefit from *their* unchangeable promise to one another. It's the same God, but a New Covenant–the Covenant He made with Abraham *before* Moses, which could not be completed until Christ came. You have no role whatsoever in the New Covenant. You are a branch. You *take* nothing from God, you simply *receive* by faith. No "name it claim it" necessary! What have you received? A new, perfect spirit! Life! Christ's life! (See Genesis 17:4, Galatians 3:16, 2:20, Hebrews 6:16-19, 7:22,25, 10:10,14, Ephesians 2:8,9, John 15:5, Colossians 3:4, 2 Corinthians 5:17, Romans 6:6-10).

A prayer for you: *Father, today I want to express my gratitude for you opening up my eyes to the difference in the Old and New Covenants. I remember being on my knees in my bedroom, begging you to take me deeper into your grace. I was so burnt out on trying harder and doing more, I was burnt out on seeing people as my enemy. All along, what I was really burnt out on was mixing the Old in with the New. I needed to go deeper. You heard my prayers and began to open up my eyes to what Jesus had truly done FOR me and TO me, so that He can live THROUGH me. Out with the Old, in with the New, He began transforming my mind! I know your timing is perfect, but I'm so grateful the period of my life in which you picked for me to go deeper into the New Covenant finally came. Please keep strengthening me as I attempt to teach the differences in the Covenants. Use my fingertips and mouth to do this properly. Give me wisdom, please. Help me to express you with gentleness and respect. Right now, I lift up all who are reading this, directly to you. I know many of them are bamboozled, as was I, when the revelation of the Old and New came to light. There's a lot to take in and their minds may be spinning. Give them a sense of peace today in knowing they have all the knowledge they'll ever need, in their hearts. It's your Spirit. Over time, you will reveal more and more! They'll go from glory to glory in understanding who you've truly recreated them to be, according to the New Covenant! We are your children! In Jesus' name I pray, amen.*

Day 5

God Isn't Trying to Kill Off Your Body

"Do you not know that your bodies are temples of the
Holy Spirit, who is in you, whom you have received
from God? You are not your own; you were bought
at a price. Therefore honor God with your bodies."

1 Corinthians 6:19,20

The Bible says our bodies are blameless—this physical shell (see 1 Thessalonians 5:23). But a lot of grace-confused Christians think we are to "sacrifice" our body each day for God. Here is the verse they'll use:

"Therefore, I urge you, brothers, in view of God's mercy, to offer your
bodies as living sacrifices, holy and pleasing to God–this is your spiritual
act of worship." (Romans 12:1)

Notice Paul says *living* sacrifice–not a dead one? And notice as he talks about our physical body being offered as a living sacrifice he says this is *spiritual* worship? This tool God has given us to walk around on planet earth–our body–is best used as spiritual worship when we are *living* our lives organically as saints. Why? Because our bodies are God's temple and *we* are fully sanctified.

We are sanctified–our spirits. Sanctified means holy. Holy means set apart. Saint means holy *person*. We are holy because God is holy and He lives *in* our bodies! (See 1 Peter 1:16). Our actions and attitudes are *being* sanctified *by* our holy spirit–who is joined with *the* Holy Spirit–as we live out our lives *naturally* as heaven-ready people! (See Hebrews 10:10, Philippians 1:6, Romans 12:2).

This is why we must be clear: God isn't trying to make us "die to self." Instead, He wants us to *be* ourselves—perfect, remade spirits. We *are* perfect, heavenly spirits *inside of* a shell made up of matter (see Hebrews 10:14, 1 Corinthians 6:19,20). We need this shell of flesh to live out this blip on the radar of eternity, of life on earth, which will determine the everlasting era of our real lives in heaven or hell.

Heavy, I know. Thankfully, as our spirits *lead* our bodies (which is worship) *rather* than the carnal desires which come from our bodies' five senses–and rather than being led by the sin *in* our physical bodies (which is inflamed by Mosaic Law observance, see Romans 7)–we are pleasing God with our choices and thoughts. I know that is a long run-on sentence, but the gist is this: Christian, just be yourself and you can't go wrong!

Who is yourself? What do *you* look like? Well, look at Jesus! Look at the fruit of His Spirit! (See Galatians 5:22,23, 1 Corinthians 13:4-8, Philippians 4:8).

By being ourselves and allowing our spirit to lead our flesh, we are walking by faith (see 2 Corinthians 5:7, Hebrews 11:6). This is cyclical because *as* you be yourself, you naturally walk by faith. On the deepest level, there is no effort here. You don't have to show effort to be who you truly are. This is why the author of Hebrews said "make every effort to *rest*" (see Hebrews 4:11). As we rest in Christ we *be* ourselves.

The truth is, not once does Paul, Peter, James, or John say that we believers have to kill ourselves, or die to self (there is a scriptural faux pas interpretation of 1 Corinthians 15, I'll get to shortly). Neither does the author of Hebrews–whether it is Paul or not–claim we have to kill off our bodies. On the contrary, many times each letter-writer said we need to *be* ourselves and if we're not, then we've forgotten who we are:

> *for it is written: "*<u>*Be*</u>* holy, because I am holy." (1 Peter 1:16)*

> *"And that is what some of you* <u>*were*</u>*. But you* <u>*were washed*</u>*, you* <u>*were sanctified*</u>*, you* <u>*were justified*</u> *in the name of the Lord Jesus Christ and by the Spirit of our God." (1 Corinthians 6:11)*

> *"But you* <u>*have*</u> *an anointing from the Holy One, and all of you* <u>*know*</u> *the truth." (1 John 2:20)*

After listing off lots of wonderful qualities of a believer, Peter even says this:

> *"But whoever lacks these traits is nearsighted to the point of blindness, having* <u>*forgotten*</u> *that he* <u>*has been cleansed*</u> *from his past sins." (2 Peter 1:9)*

Do you see these are present tense statements when each apostle references our holiness? Do you see they are *past tense* statements when referencing our non-holiness?

Our holiness *has* happened, by grace, through faith! (See Ephesians 2:8,9). Such holiness *leads* these physical bodies—not the other way around!

Further, what our physical bodies are doing or not doing isn't *causing* our holiness nor maintaining it. Our holiness comes *once* through faith which creates our supernatural rebirth! Our complete identity has changed! (See John 3:7, 2 Corinthians 5:17).

The barometer of your holiness is this: *go ahead and try to keep on sinning comfortably. It won't happen.* Why? Because your spirit is perfect and it's been recreated to *not* sin (see Romans 6:2-7).

We will live in misery when we choose to allow our bodies to act on sin. Sure, the carnal parts of these shells might get a quick thrill from it, but afterwards, it's clear that sin is not for us. Some believers live in denial all their lives of this truth, but still, such denial cannot change their spiritual DNA. You cannot be unborn from God just the same as you cannot be unborn from your momma. Birth is final, and you have no say-so in the matter! (See 2 Timothy 2:13, John 1:12, 3:6,7, 1 John 3:1,9, Hebrews 7:25).

This is why God wants us to *present* these bodies as *living* sacrifices. How? By living out our heaven-ready selves through our body! As we do, we will enjoy our lives to the fullest, as well as tap into a peace which surpasses all understanding! (See Galatians 5:22,23, John 10:10, Philippians 4:7,12,13).

So today, my friends, know this: The words "die to self" are not in the Bible. The closest thing is, "I face death every day," in 1 Corinthians 15:31. However, Paul is explaining how he faced *physical danger* while traveling to spread the gospel. Re-read this passage in context and you'll see. He even said he fought wild beasts while in Ephesus. The truth is we have a *new* self from the moment we first believe! (See Romans 6:6,7). We are not killing ourselves off little by little! Sure, our minds are being renewed to just how holy we are, but we are already complete! In my opinion, a poor translation of this verse is "I die daily." Why would I say that? Because Christians are *not* dying daily! We are living! We *have* died, and we *have been* raised back to life! Our life is now hidden with Christ in God! (See Galatians 2:20, Colossians 3:3). Our bodies are temples of His very own Spirit and we are holy! He will not dwell in unholy places! (See Colossians 1:22, 1 Corinthians 6:19).

So saint, be yourself, live your life, and *enjoy* your life! Your life is your new self combined with Christ!

A prayer for you: *Dad, today I want to thank you for teaching me the truth of my body. For so many years I thought I had to be at battle with it. I thought it was bad. I am so grateful for learning from your Spirit that you love my body and it was your very own idea! Right now, I lift up all who are reading this, directly to you. For those who have been lied to about their body, reveal the truth about it! Teach them that their body is but a tool. WE control IT, our spirits do. IT doesn't control US. Teach them that as they simply walk according to their spiritual perfection, their body will do the same a lot more often than not. Let them know you're not focused on their body, but on THEM, their everlasting selves. You're focused on their true identity, your child. As a believer, every mistake their body would ever make, Christ died for and then took it away at the Cross. His sacrifice satisfied you in full. We appreciate Him so much! In His name I pray, amen.*

How Grace Destroyed My Addiction

"For the grace of God has appeared that offers salvation to all people. It teaches us to say 'No' to ungodliness and worldly passions, and to live self-controlled, upright and godly lives in this present age"

Titus 2:11,12

"God, what have I done? Not again." I whisper as I wake up on the floor of my bedroom.

"2:25? Dang. It's gonna be a long night–and a long day." I push myself up and off the carpet, not remembering how I got there. Stumbling into the bathroom and chugging water from the faucet as if I've never drank water before, Satan begins pounding my mind with a sledgehammer, "Just look at you! *Fake Christian!* You did it again! You're still half-drunk, don't fall over, idiot. You'll never break that addiction."

Cottonmouth, heart palpitations, demonic accusations and suicidal levels of anxiety–these were just a few of the side effects from my binge drinking.

But, "Don't tell me what to do! I'm a successful business owner and I have a *huge* Facebook ministry! I *know* how to control my drinking, so back off!"

My thought patterns were so off-kilter when it came to mature alcohol consumption that "having a few" was a joke. Those of us who constantly have to question ourselves *about* this addiction? We have no clue how to control how much we drink–and we know it. So, we get angry when people question us about it.

Those who love us, *love* us, that's why they call us out on it. They shouldn't have to be afraid of our binge drinking, no matter if we *are* providing for them. When they finally set healthy boundaries for us, recovery has a much better chance of happening. If that's you, stand up to the person who keeps getting drunk, but do it with love and respect. Never stop standing up.

The great obsession of men and women who struggle with the tendency of alcoholism is this: We want to control and enjoy our drinking, like the normal-drinking people. But when we control our drinking, we can't enjoy it; and when we enjoy it, we can't control it. So the cycle continues until the day we realize we can *never* have a single drop.

This is heartbreaking for a person in love with the drink. The break-up with alcohol is a tough one and can only be accomplished authentically through God's grace. Without grace, we white-knuckle it. We pull ourselves up by our bootstraps. We expect *everyone* to never drink again–especially around us, "How dare you! You know I struggle with that!" We dread going places where there's alcohol, we shut off the world and miss our addiction like a baby misses their binky. We feel sorry for ourselves and long for the day we can drink again.

Grace, however, obliterates that stupid crap. It teaches us who we truly are as God's children: *sober, confident, enthusiastic saints who enjoy life to the fullest. Slaves to nothing except for God's righteousness.* You can easily point out someone who has *not* gotten sober by way of grace–they think they're better than those who are still fighting to break free. Giving victory lessons is their favorite thing to do, but it's only a matter of time before they fall again. I should know because that was me for a year and a half, when I got sober by my own effort, 14 years go. Relapse was the result.

I've been a Christian since single digit age, what I didn't realize was even in the midst of my battle with alcohol, God never left me. The grace-confused people who binged on legalanity had me convinced I wasn't saved because of my heavy drinking. However, God taught me that I *struggled* with drinking *because* I was saved. The conflict was the proof!

Getting drunk all the time would never match up with my perfect, heaven-ready spirit–my *true* identity. I could still be drinking to this day, and nothing could ever change the fact that God gave me a new spirit when I was a boy. From the moment I first believed Jesus forgave me, I was supernaturally crucified with Him, buried with Him, and then *resurrected* with Him. We became combined *despite* what this physical shell of flesh would ever do or *not* do again (see Romans 6:6,7, Galatians 2:20, 1 Corinthians 6:17,19, 1 John 4:13, Colossians 3:3).

My mind had to be renewed to this truth. Drinking until I was smashed, quite often, was the same as holding my head under water until I passed out. It made no sense–*but* it couldn't alter who I *was*, and still am.

How could I possibly get sober though? I had literally tried over a thousand times, read lots of books, never missed an episode of Intervention; I recommitted *daily*, seen counselors, got prayed over, walked the isle–I even had multiple accountability partners and did *all* of the AA Steps. Never could I pull it off!

"WHAT IS WRONG WITH ME?!" was a regular expression of mine. Nothing was wrong with me. In fact, everything was right with me– not with my actions, but with *me*. Christ had made me right, once and for all time (see Hebrews 10:10,14, Romans 6:10). My problem was, the same self-determined effort I used to accomplish the American Dream would *not* work for this. I had to give up on trying–which *I* could do better than anyone– and I had to start trusting God's grace.

I managed this sinful activity of closet binge drinking very well. It's not like I was living in a sleeping bag, begging for booze money on the corner with a *God Bless* sign. But–I was no better, or worse, than such a person. I didn't understand the power which would come *to* me, through the grace that was already *in* me. It would be this grace dispensed from God that would *teach me* how to live a sober, self-controlled, enjoyable life.

After hearing such a thing, a behavior-focused person might say, "Greasy grace, Matt! *Greasy* grace! You're just using grace as an excuse to tell others they can live in sin! If you were *truly* saved, then you would have *truly* repented and never touched alcohol again! Alcohol harms many people!"

Friend, really? That's what you're going with? Alcohol harms many people just like *guns* harm many people. Think about it. Alcohol and guns aren't the problem, it's the minds *behind* them *handling* them–minds which must be renewed by God's grace.

After all, Jesus' first recorded miracle exposed His taste for *good* wine (see John 2:1-11). Our Creator is a wine connoisseur, not a grape juice lover. It's not the wine that's the issue, it's being controlled by a liquid. There's nothing wrong with alcohol, but there *is* something wrong with being obsessed over it, or depending on it for what God has already given to us through Jesus' Spirit: love, joy, peace, fulfillment, identity, and purpose.

Paul said don't get *drunk* on wine, proving the wine mentioned in the Bible is not Welch's (see Ephesians 5:18). He also recommended to Timothy that he *stop* drinking so much water, and instead, drink some wine for his frequent stomach problems (see 1 Timothy 5:23). So why is it certain religious people want to die on the hill of, "Wine wasn't fermented in the Bible!"?

Simple. It messes with their behavior-focused theology of, "Be like me, or else you'll burn!"

If their *Savior*, Christ Himself, actually caught a buzz, then their entire house of legalistic cards would tumble over. Case in point:

I was walking through Wal-Mart after work, not too long ago, to pick up dinner ingredients. While there, I saw a man I recognized from a local church whom I'd just met. I own an alarm company and recently had a meeting in front of a large group of church board members–to present my products–and *he* was one of those faces in the crowd.

They ended up voting on going with my company, and not only purchased a security system, but also a video surveillance package. I was very happy about this so I hung out for a while, chumming it up after the sale, and I talked to this man briefly. Now here he was coming toward me at the supermarket with something tucked up under his coat.

"Hey! How are you?" I said with a smile, not remembering his name.

Stopping quickly, caught off guard and inspecting his surroundings, "Oh…I'm fine."

Half-surprised at who I was–but recognizing me by my Alarm Security polo–the man captured me gazing down at his jacket. "Whatcha got there?" I questioned him kindly.

"This? Oh, it's just some Saint James wine. It's my favorite. I have to hide it in case one of those Bible-thumpers see me here with it."

I burst out loud laughing! And he did too, but with a hint of nervousness. Chuckling in my reply, "I hear you! Well, you take care now," and off I went toward the back.

Friend, do you see it? This particular denomination in which this man attends, preaches that wine *isn't* fermented. Why? Because they don't want to believe Jesus ever *really* drank alcohol, which is a lie. Because *then* that would mean we are free to drink–or not drink–it's up to us. They want to put a law on the bottle so their members won't go "wild in sin" but look at what such a law is doing? Exiting *in* this man *what* he was told *not* to do. Law inflames sin! It stirs it up! It doesn't control it! (See Romans 7:8). Only freedom through grace allows us to live healthy, well-balanced lives.

This board member *from that church* was hiding a bottle of wine because his conscience–which was deceiving him through bad teaching–was incorrectly *convicting* him of sin. God's Spirit does not *convict* Christians of sin, but of our righteousness (see 2 Corinthians 5:21). Only the unbelievers *of this world* are convicted of sin by the Holy Spirit (see John 16:18). *We* are being *counseled* by God–*not* convicted. We're being counseled *into* grace, *through* grace, and *by* grace (see John 14:26, Titus 2:11,12).

So what would set this man free from hiding his nice bottle of wine? ... Grace. Realizing he is free. It was for freedom that Christ set us free–*by* grace! (See Galatians 5:1, Ephesians 2:8,9). Right now, he's addicted to legalism and church laws; impressing the hierarchies and trying to appear more holy to the "sub-Christians." Grace would destroy those addictions too.

It is the grace of God that teaches us how to live upright, godly lives–not church rules, not twisting Scripture to our denominational liking–but God's undeserved kindness. The truth is, we are allowed to drink the same amount Jesus drank. But if we're being led by His Spirit to *not* drink, then we should give it up because He knows what's best for us. He's not trying to keep something *from* us, His desire is to set us free from mental strongholds.

Grace is not greasy *or* cheap! It's our firm foundation and the most expensive thing *ever*–for Jesus, not us! For us it's completely free! Because of grace, if

I had never quit drinking, and my unrenewed thoughts continued to lead me down the path of alcoholism, I'd *still* have God infused with my spirit! I'd *still* be saved! I'd still be His child forever!

Jesus didn't say, "It is finished! *Unless* you get addicted to a liquid, then it's *un*finished! I'm out!"

No. He'd never leave me…ever. The promise He made to the Father at the Cross and my one-time belief in it would not allow such a thing to happen. I could swim in my favorite beer, 24 hours a day, and be drunk for the rest of my life–*still*, my identity would never change because of the New Covenant. I am holy and there's nothing I can do to change this because of the blood of Jesus *once* poured out for me (see Hebrews 1:3).

If I was hungover right now, and today was my first day of sobriety, I'd be just as righteous and blameless as I'd been since the moment I first believed. *All* of my drunken episodes had been washed away–past, present, and future. I have no control over altering or improving that washing by way of my actions and attitudes (see Colossians 1:22, 3:3, 2 Corinthians 5:21, 1 Corinthians 6:11).

God never confuses our behavior with our identity. We can build a thousand churches or be a pastor for nearly all our life and *not* be His kid. We could be addicted for 50 years, fail at marriage five times, or murder our unborn baby, and *be* His kid. Identity matters to our Creator–our heart. Is it a new heart? Does He live there? As His kids, yes, and yes. We've inherited *His* sinless Spirit–His Holy Spirit–but not just that. We've also been *given* a brand new holy spirit of our own! We are combined with God like a handkerchief in water–separate, yet one (see John 1:12, Romans 6:6,7, 2 Corinthians 5:17, Colossians 3:3, 1 Corinthians 6:19).

Grace empowers us. Grace says, "If you live for 110 years, struggling with a particular sin pattern, you're still a coheir with Christ, and you can't change this."

Grace is Jesus. You can replace the word *grace* in every spot in the Bible with the word *Jesus*–and vice versa–and the same impact would be made. The same point, the same outcome, according to the gospel. This is why Paul called the gospel, the gospel *of* grace (see Acts 20:24).

Grace says you will never be punished for sinning because *Jesus* was punished for your sinning. Grace says you are enough *exactly* as you are. Grace will never leave you nor forsake you. Grace is preparing an amazing spot for you–a position in eternity–*as* you read this sentence. And for those of us who have struggled with alcohol? Grace has taken all of our sins away, every drunken mistake, every celebratory night turned nightmare, every regret. Grace has banished those embarrassing times into oblivion, as far as the east is from the west (see Psalm 103:12, Hebrews 8:12).

So today, my friends, know this: Grace will destroy your addiction! The sufficiency of God's grace is all you need to break any bad habit! *One* of my addictions was alcohol. From the moment I first tasted it and felt that release, I was hooked. For 17 years, I thought I could never live without it, I thought I could never truly enjoy myself. Those were lies coming from demonic forces, the power of sin, and my immature thinking. The truth is, life is so much better without it! Yes, some people can have a few and be done, but that never worked for me. Every once in a while I might be able to pull it off, but those times were few and far between. With over four years of sobriety now, I can say that God's grace has not only empowered me to never drink another drop, but also to enjoy who I really am! I am His child! And so are you, if you believe Jesus has forgiven you! If you haven't–then believe! Believe, and begin enjoying His grace today!

A prayer for you: *Heavenly Father, what an amazing day it is! It's not an anniversary or a specific day to celebrate something–BUT MY LIFE IS AMAZING! It's amazing because of your grace! Every single DAY is amazing, even when my circumstances are not, because I'm enjoying your grace at all times! IT IS GOOOOOOOOOD! Right now, I lift up all who are reading this, directly to you. Dad, so many of them are struggling with an addiction, they are distraught and close to giving up on hope. You know who they are, and you're speaking to their hearts right now. Help them come to know your grace–who is Jesus–on such a deep level, no amount of ANYTHING could convince them they aren't perfectly secure IN Him. You aren't looking for them to clean up their act–or even to be cleaned up by you. You're looking to give them life! An abundant life! Christ's life! If they believe, they already have Him, they just need to let Him come out! If they don't, then they can receive Him this very moment by believing He has forgiven them of their sins. Please destroy ungraceful mindsets today. Please destroy addictions through your grace–whatever addiction it may be. Thank you, Father. In Jesus' name I pray, amen.*

Day 7

Works, Obedience, and Commitment

*"Even though Jesus was God's Son, he learned
obedience from the things he suffered."*

Hebrews 5:8

Jesus *learned* obedience, yet He never sinned, and *we* are His ambassadors (see 2 Corinthians 5:20). Think about that for a moment. I gotta say, it's a strange thing representing our Creator, is it not?

Thankfully, we too–like Christ while here in the flesh–learn and grow each day (see Luke 2:52). And like Him, we don't *change,* as Christians. We've already *been* changed! We've been made brand new! The supernatural fabric of our being is exactly like Jesus'! (See 2 Corinthians 5:17,21, Romans 6:6,7, Galatians 2:20, 1 John 4:17).

So instead of changing, we mature into our real selves. Our actions and attitudes start to line up with our holy spirit who is meshed together with *the* Holy Spirit (see Romans 12:2, Philippians 1:6, 1 Corinthians 6:17). When I began to understand this truth, I stopped praying, "God, change me!" and I *started* praying, "God, take me deeper into the knowledge of your grace. Show me more about who I am."

Just the same as our original ancestors, we can be tempted greatly to shift our focus onto Satan's knowledge of good and evil (see Genesis 3:4,5). Therefore, taking our focus off of our heavenly identity. We *think* we want to point out right and wrong, but that's not our job. Our job is to believe and then *be*. Such a two-part sentence can be a dinner bell for religious demons who call themselves "Discernment." However, from this natural state of holiness, error is pushed up and out, gently. We put away our meat cleaver of self-righteousness and stop chopping away at our sin, as well as the sin of others. Only by sheathing our sin-knife will heavenly attributes begin sprouting from us without effort (see Galatians 5:22,23, 1 Corinthians 13:4-8, Philippians 4:8).

When our sin-consciousness graduates to our righteousness-consciousness, wisdom, ripeness, and readiness explode from within.

To be clear, *is* there a such thing as good and evil? Of course. But rather than attempt to straighten everyone out—or worse, tell them, "I'm your best example!"—we should be concentrating on pointing to Jesus. This is where the sweet spot is found; a lush, green pasture entered through a narrow gate. Jesus *is* that gate (see John 10:9). Conservatism isn't, cleaning up our act isn't, praising a man riding around in a clear, bulletproof car isn't. Only Jesus is.

If we will blame absolutely everything on the Cross, all of the "Yeah, buts" aren't too difficult to deal with. By doing so, we can easily dissolve the excuses as to why God is *not* really that great. He gave His Son for us. I can't say that most would do the same.

Also, most confrontations will go smoothly (on your part) because there is *no* pressure on you. None. You really don't even have anything to defend, but instead, to express. The amazing truth of the gospel is this: *pressure does not come from Christ.* Easiness does. Organic behavior does. Rest does (see Matthew 11:28-30, 2 Peter 1:5-9, Hebrews 4:11).

For a saint–anyone who has placed their faith in Jesus one time–pressure is a red flag to pause, take a step back, and scan the situation. "Why am I feeling this way? Where is this coming from? Am I trying, or trusting?"

Pressure usually comes from our old ways of thinking and coping which haven't yet been renewed by the Spirit within us; or demonic forces, or people who struggle with religion, or even the power of sin. But *not* from Jesus. He is God and self-sufficient, not *needing* anything from us (see Acts 17:25). We've been invited to a house for a pleasant gathering where the owner isn't handing out aprons. Relax. Enjoy. Be yourself (see Luke 14:13-23, 10:38-42).

When we don't add anything to the finished work of the Cross and we *point* to what *it* has done, all of our great "works," "obedience," and "commitment" become authentic. Parentheses surround those three words for a reason, as in, they may or may not be what they seem. It all depends on *who* we are reflecting in the midst of them.

When we aren't expressing Jesus, nor fixated on the Cross alone, all of our works, obedience, and commitment are actually repellents. As painful as it may be to our ears, nobody wants to be like us when we act like we're doing something better than them. Therefore, the mindset of, *"I'm focused on the Cross,"* will take our ego, yank it by the collar, boot it in the pants and say, "Go kick rocks! You're not needed here!"

Friend, when we aren't allowing love to come from our roots, where Christ is, this topic about spiritual disciplines can become fighting words. For Christians, the phrase "spiritual disciplines" is an oxymoron. Christ was already disciplined *for* us–both spiritually and physically. Is God now disciplining us when we read our Bibles, pray, and do good works? No. We aren't being disciplined in regard to such things. Instead, we are being *discipled* by these actions– we are being *counseled* by doing this stuff (see Matthew 28:19, John 14:26).

If you never read your Bible again, pray another word, or do a good thing for the rest of your life, God would not discipline you for this. The discipline which occurred at the Cross was suffice. Sure, you'll feel like a clogged pipe because you're denying yourself of expressing your relationship with God, but you won't be put in the corner nor shamed by Him. Your shame was put on Jesus, all of it. *You* are enough.

Sadly, many of us have misplaced our identity in works, obedience, and commitment "to" God, rather than just enjoying Him. These are the same mistakes the Israelites made in the first Covenant. We try to make others think they need to do *this* commandment and *that* law, so they can be like us. We are measuring people by *ourselves*. This is a mirage. This is fool's gold. This is becoming *un*-focused on the Cross and falling *away* from the mindset of grace (see Galatians 5:4). Not *from* grace–because grace won't allow that–but from the *pleasure* of basking in it. Paul explains this stumbling block to the Corinthians:

> "We do not dare to classify or compare ourselves with some who commend themselves. When they measure themselves <u>by themselves</u> and compare themselves <u>with themselves, they are not wise</u>." (2 Corinthians 10:12)

By taking our gaze off of Christ, our "level" (there's those quotations again) of works, obedience, and commitment is threatened. The next step is to stress out, prove ourselves right, or to become furious while attempting to protect our fake jewels. So let's break down all three of these topics and button this up.

As for our works, if they aren't coming by way of grace, they mean nothing. Paul penned this to the Romans:

> "And if by grace, then it cannot be based on works; if it were, grace would no longer be grace." (Romans 11:6)

Do you see the switch there? The flip-flop? I missed this Good News Easter-Egg for *so* long. Because of being compared to the works of others *by* others–either blatantly or passive-aggressively–along with me having an ultra-competitive, alpha personality, I wasn't enjoying the grace within me in order *to* express organic works. I was being bamboozled by dark forces egging me on to be "better" than other Christians. That's not possible, we are all the same in God's eyes (see Romans 2:11, Acts 10:34).

As for obedience? What you are about to read will upset those who battle with the tendency of legalanity, yet obedience-hounders receive the most simple explanation *ever* from the New Testament. Ready for this? According to the gospel, obedience is *believing*. Just look at this:

"Through him we received grace and apostleship to call all the Gentiles to the obedience that comes from faith for his name's sake." (Romans 1:5)

And again, toward the end of Romans:

"but now revealed and made known through the prophetic writings by the command of the eternal God, so that all the Gentiles might come to the obedience that comes from faith" (Romans 16:26)

Gentiles is everyone on this planet who isn't Jewish. Everyone. But even the Jews had to be re-grafted back *into* the New Covenant through the obedience of faith alone in Christ as the Messiah. Moses had to go. The temple had to go. Animal sacrifices at the Day of Atonement to get their annual forgiveness of sin from the priests *had* to go (see Hebrews 10:26). Many of them refused and were *not* included with Christ as *we* now are as believers who were formerly Gentiles (see Galatians 3:28). Their Jewish lineage no longer meant anything, all that mattered was new creations in

Christ. But they didn't care because they wanted stuff to do, rather than simply obey by faith.

"Those dirty Gentiles aren't holy like us! You're just giving people a license to sin, Paul!"

The truth was, Paul, as a formerly devout Pharisee, fully understood that *they* were all sinning just fine *without* a license (see 1 Timothy 1:12-17, Philippians 3:3-9, Romans 7). The Law that they believed was making them righteous was doing nothing except exposing the dirt on their faces. The Mosaic Law was like an x-ray machine, not causing broken bones, but pointing them out–not causing sin, but exposing it. He knew they needed a better way, a way which comes *only* by obedience through faith–a way their very Scriptures foretold about: Jesus (see John 5:39,40).

Unfortunately, this continues on today as they wail at a wall, sticking prayer notes into the cracks and begging God for stuff all while ignoring *what* that wall represented: *the need for a Savior.* The wailing is over! The Messiah is *here!* Without faith in Christ alone, apart from the Law–ALL OF IT–they too are without hope, just as the Gentiles were in the Old Covenant (see Hebrews 10:28,29, Romans 11:11-31, Ephesians 2:11-22).

And for the last subject of the title of this devotional, commitment? With all due respect to every person reading this: YOUR COMMITMENT TO GOD IS A JOKE. So is mine. Humanity is the worst promise keepers ever created and that's why Jesus had to die. Thankfully, *thankfully,* the New Covenant has nothing to do with *our* commitment, but instead, God's commitment to God, and our belief in the need to benefit *from* that commitment.

God's commitment to God? Yes! The Father to the Son and the Son to the Father! *This* commitment, this *promise,* was made at the Cross! (See John 19:30, Hebrews 6:16-20, Romans 5:1).

So what's our role? As much angst as this will cause our old mindsets, our *only* role is to reach out, hands wide open, and say, "Thank you." We don't reach out and *take* it, we *receive it* by faith, once (see Ephesians 2:8,9, Hebrews 10:10, Romans 6:10).

This is the New Covenant. The Old Covenant was established between God and the people group of Israel–whom Moses just freed from Egypt–at the base of Mount Sinai. 613 contingencies in which the Jews said, "We will do all of it!" (Ten of those 613 were the Ten Commandments). Moses then went back up the mountain, head shaking with eyebrows raised, informing God, "Yep. They said they'll do it" (see Exodus 19:8). God already knew they agreed before Moses expressed this to Him, but Moses still had to *complete* this Covenant because he was the Old Covenant's mediator. Jesus is the mediator for the new one! (See Hebrews 9:15, 1 Timothy 2:5).

Do you see the basis of the Old? *They agreed to it, God never forced them.* Do you see the basis of the New? *Christ agreed to it, the Father never forced Him.* So for *this* Covenant we've become the beneficiaries to *their* promise, by faith, *not* by being promise keepers of the Law, which required perfection (Matthew 5:48, James 2:10, Galatians 3:10).

What a relief!

It's the *same* God, but a *new* agreement! (See Hebrews 8:6,13). Was there anything wrong with the Old Covenant? No! It was perfect! It *is* perfect. But it never *perfected* anyone by obeying it. The fault was found in the Jews' inability to live up to their end of the bargain–what *they* agreed to, not God (see Hebrews 8:7, Romans 3:11,20, 7:12, Galatians 2:16).

In His great love and mercy, He took them *out* of the equation and inserted Himself, and then invited everyone. The good news of the gospel is *He* will never break a covenant like we do. *His* commitment to *us* is too great.

It's His commitment–not ours–which is the most amazing part of what we enjoy. As His children, even when we *think* we've become faithless, He remains faithful. Why? Because He cannot disown Himself and He doesn't have the ability to lie (see 2 Timothy 2:13, Hebrews 13:5, John 10:28, Titus 1:2).

So today, my friends, know this: Just enjoy the Cross. Enjoy peace. He is enough and so are you. As a believer, Jesus Christ is infused with your very own spirit. *He* will produce all good works *through* you, He will be *obedient* through you, and He will be *committed* through you. Your old spirit died and you got a new one which has literally been placed inside of Him. It's not "all of Jesus and none of you"—oh no. It's both of you. It's a relationship. It's a branch and a vine. So be yourself! Live out who you really are! As you do, you will always enjoy good works, obedience, and commitment, together as a team! (See John 15:5, Romans 6:6,7, 2 Corinthians 5:17, Galatians 2:20, Colossians 1:22, 3:3, 1 Corinthians 6:17,19, Hebrews 10:10,14).

A prayer for you: *Heavenly Father, today I want to thank you for revealing the truth of your grace to me. Take me even deeper and never stop. Right now, I lift up all who are reading this, directly to you. Dad, so many of them are on the brink of just giving up, and that's okay. When we finally give up on trying to impress you—or to keep what you've freely given to us through the Cross—we fall backwards, into the abyss of your grace. This free-fall has no end and it is lined with the most authentic euphoria known to any created being. Pressure, guilt, condemnation, hierarchies, shame, fear—and more—all get smaller and smaller into the distance as we lay back looking up with arms wide open…falling…falling…falling through wave upon wave upon wave of your love. This is what you planned for us all along. Love. Grace. Relationship…We look forward to falling into this chasm, for eternity. Amen.*

Day 8

What Does It Mean to Be Free?

"So if the Son sets you free, you will
be free indeed." ~Jesus

John 8:36

Today is July 4th, 2018! The day our country celebrates its freedom! But what does it mean to *truly* be free? We have many freedoms as Americans—many more than most of the countries of this world. But what does freedom mean? We all have an opinion about this subject.

Is real freedom the right to act on my sexual desires however I see fit?

Is freedom the ability to speak my mind without worry of imprisonment?

Is freedom enjoying and showing God's grace–unless I have to give this grace away to those who disagree with me politically?

Maybe true freedom is *financial* freedom?

Then again, we might call freedom, "freedom from an addiction" or "freedom from a relationship."

Is real freedom the freedom to practice a religion? Or freedom to believe in nothing at all?

What does it mean to be free? ... Paul told the Galatians this:

> "It is for freedom that Christ has set us free. Stand firm, then, and do not let yourselves be burdened again by a yoke of slavery." (Galatians 5:1)

What was the heavy, uncomfortable yoke he was referring to? Legalism. Attempting to improve their status with God through Mosaic Law observance. The church in Galatia had gotten bored with faith in Christ alone and needed their ears tickled–they needed to be told to *do* something else. We modern-day American Christians do the same thing when we have a laundry list of "things to do and not do" to improve our faith.

For us, WE. ARE. FREE–we are *already* free, and there's nothing else we can do to cause ourselves to be more free. I'm not talking about our physical bodies—although those are free too—but I'm talking about *us*, you and I, believer. We are literally *free* spirits.

Our spirit is free from the power of sin.

I know that sounds religious, and it preaches good when people say this from the pulpit, but I'm not talking about sinful actions and attitudes. I'm talking about the *force* of sin–not the *verbs* of sin (these verbs are better known as "sinning"). The actual *power* of sin is what we are truly free from!

From the moment we first believed Jesus forgave us, our spirit was literally crucified with Christ in the spiritual realm, buried, and then raised back to life as a new, perfect, *sinless* spirit, who is forever enmeshed with Christ's own Spirit. We got a brand new spirit! Look:

> "I have been crucified with Christ and I no longer live, but Christ lives in me. The life I now live in the body, I live by faith in the Son of God, who loved me and gave himself for me." (Galatians 2:20)

The first *I* in that verse is our old, sinful spirit. The second *I* is our new, sinless spirit! Here's more proof:

> "*For we know that <u>our old self was crucified with him</u> so that the body ruled by sin <u>might be done away with</u>, that we should <u>no longer be slaves to sin</u>—because anyone who <u>has died</u> has been <u>set free from sin</u>. Now if we died with Christ, we believe that <u>we will also live with him</u>.*"
> (*Romans 6:6-8*)

Paul is not talking about later on in heaven–HE'S TALKNG ABOUT NOW! This stuff *has happened*–past tense–to every single believer equally! We have been set free from the power of sin and placed inside of God forever! We are new creations *inside of* Christ!

> "*Therefore, if anyone <u>is in Christ</u>, the new creation <u>has come</u>: The old <u>has gone</u>, the new <u>is here</u>!*" (*2 Corinthians 5:17*)

> "*For you <u>died</u>, and your life is now <u>hidden with Christ in God</u>.*"
> (*Colossians 3:3*)

Friend, it doesn't matter if you felt it–it happened. Our salvation–the receiving of our new, sinless spirit–is not based on our feelings or exuding a supernatural gift. It's based on our faith in Jesus' ability to forgive us once and for all time (see Hebrews 7:25, 10:10, Ephesians 2:8,9). Believing this truth sets us free from the power of sin, right now, not later on when our physical shell wears out.

This might be difficult to understand because the modern American church has attempted to make us believe we are free from sin when we stop sinning, or when we sin less. This is not what Paul was referencing in Romans

6 (nor was he talking about water when he said "baptized into Christ"–not once does he mention a liquid). With such an incorrect theology of "you're completely forgiven of your sin until you sin" fear and hypocrisy runs rampant. Paul was talking about the *force* of sin.

When Adam and Eve chose to no longer believe God about their perfect identity, and instead were sold on the "knowledge" of good and evil by Satan, a power entered into our physical realm called *sin* (see Romans 5:12). Like gravity, it's everywhere. Even as a believer, it's still a parasite in our physical bodies (see Romans 7)–not in our spirits, but in our flesh.

Sin is the batter that Satan and his demonic morons use to cook up ideas in our mind which will lead us toward ungodly choices and thinking. From the opening book of the Bible, we are warned about the power of sin:

> "Sin is crouching at your door; it desires to have you, but you must rule over it." (See Genesis 4:7)

Do you see that sin is an *it*?

Jesus said we are *really* only slaves when we are slaves to sin (see John 8:34). But *then* He makes the claim that He Himself can set us free from this crippling power! (John 8:36). How? Only through a new spiritual birth into the family of God, by grace through faith.

He tried to explain this very thing to a very legalistic man as they met up under the cloak of night so his religious buddies wouldn't find out:

> Don't be surprised when I say, "You must be born again." (John 3:7)

When we *act on* this supernatural force in our flesh, we *create* the verbs of sin—or "sinning." Thankfully, for those who believe in the power of the Cross, Jesus has taken all of our sins committed *away*–past, present, and future!

How is this possible? Because He is not bound by time like us! (See John 1:29, 1 John 3:5, 2 Peter 3:8). Further, just because the power of sin suggests something, that doesn't mean we have to act on it, therefore bringing it to life through our physical members: our hands, feet, mouth, and even our brain.

We are dead to this power and alive in Christ! (See Romans 6:11). We are holy, blameless, and set *apart* from sin! (See Colossians 1:22). So we don't have to *act* like slaves to sin. That's what we are doing when we chose *to* sin—we are acting. Christians are *not* slaves to sin, we are free! Paul said:

> "But thanks be to God that, though you <u>used to be slaves to sin</u>, you have become obedient <u>from the heart</u>…You <u>have been</u> set free from sin and <u>have become slaves to righteousness</u>." (See Romans 6:17,18)

SLAVES TO RIGHTEOUSNESS?! I need to repeat that: *slaves* to righteousness? Slaves means you have no choice in the matter! Christian, do you see it? Do you *see* that your new birth *has caused you* to become a new creation who is shackled to rightness with God?! You are chained to holiness!

YOUR SPIRIT IS BOUND UP IN GODLY PERFECTION FOREVER! (See Hebrews 10:14).

How?!…Only by way of what Jesus did at the Cross. Only by way of a supernatural rebirth. Only by way of receiving a new, sinless spirit, who is connected to the Holy Spirit of Jesus Christ. Not by what you do or don't do, but by who you are, your new identity; by your one-time spiritual death and resurrection, *now*, not later. The only new thing that will happen later is you will get a new *physical* body (like Jesus' new physical body) and the power of sin will be banished forever (see 1 Corinthians 15:52, Hebrews 9:28, Revelation 21:4).

Christian, you are complete as of now (see Colossians 2:9,10). You are free, as of *now*. Therefore, live free.

So today, my friends, know this: True freedom is being free from sin—the power. True freedom is walking *out* our identity of not allowing this power to come to life through our actions and attitudes. True freedom is realizing *we* rule over sin–not the other way around. We are dead to it! Freedom is knowing that sin has no authority over us! True freedom is coming to the knowledge that even when we don't walk according to our true nature—sinless, righteous, holy spirits—the Cross will never allow the power of sin to have any dominion over who we are! We are free, Christian! We have the deepest level of freedom on all the earth, not just in America! Enjoy it and live it out!

A prayer for you: *Heavenly Father, thank you for true freedom. Thank you for my new self, my new identity, and my new family. You brought me into your family by faith when I was just a young boy, but since then you've taught me what it truly means to be your child. Thank you, Dad. Right now, I lift up all who are reading this, directly to you. For those who don't understand what you've done to their spirits, reveal the truth to them. Let them know you've recreated them in your Son if they believe He has forgiven them! Let them know such a belief has set them free from the power of sin and is irreversible! Reveal their true identity today! Reveal the infiniteness of your grace which is the basis of our freedom! In Christ's name I pray, amen.*

Day 9

Stop Trying so Hard to Be a Christian

"Let us therefore strive to enter that rest"

See Hebrews 4:11

"Are you going to go to sleep any time soon?" my wife asks me as I'm up way past my bed time, going back and forth in the comments section of a Facebook post.

"Yeah. But I really want this atheist to know God loves them. I wanna be sure to answer all of their questions even if they're rude to me. I'm sure they gave up on knowing God because a Christian was rude to *them*, so I want to be extra nice and not write them off."

On into the hours, I proceed to reply to each comment past midnight, until I felt they *might* be satisfied with all my answers. *"If I can get them to like me, maybe they'll give God a chance,"* was how I was thinking.

Because of my Facebook theology session in which I mustered up all of my "amazing" religious vigor–but not legalistic "of course"–I only got a few hours of sleep and was very tired the next day. But I "witnessed hard" and I was "gently" expressing the love of Christ.

I'm writing in lots of quotation marks because who *knows* what that person thought after the hours-long social media exchange. But my camouflaged religious pride sure was puffed up the next day. After all, I did it "kindly," I did "work" for the Lord. Sure, God can use this kind of effort. He can even use error to bring people to Him (see Philippians 1:15-18). So what's the big deal that I'm making here?

My problem was this: I was trying way too hard to do something that should have just come natural.

And maybe, if I was, I might not have said *anything* in that post to the atheist. Let alone spend hours going back and forth. Or I might have said one thing and dropped it–or two or three things. There is no litmus test. It's not *effort* that does work for God, but resting. When we rest, we are doing the most natural thing we can possibly do as holy people.

It was years ago when this event happened, and at the time, I was trying to "get" people to place their faith in Jesus. I had believed the lie of the enemy, that it was *my* job to save the world. It's *not* my job to save the world. That's God's job. Such talk will stir up the chatter of the devil in many religious people's minds. Those who are incorrectly finding their identity in church work, Scripture memorization, appeasing church leaders, knocking on doors, mission trips, or expressing supernatural gifts–they won't like this topic. It angers the unrenewed parts of their thinking.

However, it was for freedom that Christ set us free! (See Galatians 5:1). It wasn't for witnessing. It wasn't for studying the Bible. It wasn't for taking pictures with poverty-stricken kids in third world countries. It wasn't for having a huge social media ministry or writing multiple books about Jesus.

I did not know this. I thought that if I was uber-nice and spent tons of time explaining what I believed about God *then* other people would become

Christian, *then* God would see me glow, *then* He'd be pleased as punch with me. It was draining. It was stressful. Worst of all, I never knew if I was *truly* doing enough. Where was the tipping point and how could I be absolutely sure?

I had done all this stuff–I had *stopped* all this supposed "bad stuff"–I had read all this stuff, and produced all this stuff, yet angst was still leading my thought life each day.

"Do more! Be more! There's more! That's not enough! Stay hungry! Be radical! Get pumped up for Jesus and stay pumped! Be like me, I have tons of spiritual disciplines! This is what *you* need to do!"

…Oy vey. Where is this *rest* Christ talked about so often? I want *that*.

My Christian life was way out of balance, and this is no way to live. Yes, my intentions were good–and Christ was in me in full–but I was putting all of the pressure on *actions* rather than simply relax in who I already *was*. I wouldn't let Christ just be Christ through me. I had been taught it was my God-given duty to make disciples of disciples. But when Jesus said "go make disciples," He was not saying to *force* ourselves, but instead to *be* ourselves.

Then, one day I read this verse. It changed everything for me in regard to my stress-filled Christian life:

> *"Let us therefore strive to enter that rest"* (See Hebrews 4:11)

In context, that *rest* is Jesus. The author of Hebrews was writing a group of people who worked extremely hard to please God through what they did and didn't do–just like I was. He, or she, was letting the Hebrew people know the *only* thing they should be striving for is to enter the rest of faith in Christ alone.

"But I already have that," I said to myself. *"It can't be that easy."*

So I looked up Hebrews 4:11 in other translations of the Bible:

> *"Therefore let us be diligent to enter that rest"*

"So let us <u>do our best</u> to enter that rest."

"<u>make every effort</u> to enter that rest"

"Make every *effort* to *rest*?! How is this possible?! How can you put forth an effort to relax?! I don't get it, God?!"

"Just be yourself." I could hear His words in my spirit. Not in an audible voice, but in a *knowing* in a *motivation*. It was starting to make sense! Because of Hebrews 4:11, the Spirit of Christ began to open up my eyes to some *other* verses. Verses I've read many times before, but just *now* realized what they meant:

> *"I am the vine; you are the branches. If you remain in me and I in you,*
> *you will bear much fruit; apart from me you can do nothing."*
> *(John 15:5)*

The legalistic teaching I heard all of my life used this verse as a threat of hell for Christians who weren't "doing enough" for God. But that's not what it means! This is a *description* of who we already are! It's not a *pre*-scription of the Christian life, as in, "You better bear much fruit or you're not abiding!" No! This is a *de*-scription of what we naturally do as we live our lives! Jesus is explaining how and *what* we will produce–organically–not by Mosaic legislation, guilt, threats of hell, or force!

Jesus is the vine whom the branches *do* remain in! The branches are not responsible for straining to produce fruit *or* stay connected to the vine! ALL THE BRANCH DOES IS LIVE ITS LIFE!

It is the *vine* that provides the branch's sustenance to even be *able* to produce fruit! What is the branch doing? It is witnessing hard? Is it stressing out trying to be sure it's made the vine Savior *and* Lord? Is it begging daily for forgiveness so the vine hangs on to it? Are different branches being held to different standards? Is the branch going to seminary and conferences so the vine approves of its theology? Is it calling out all of the false branches—as if the vine cannot tell? Is it opening up another church? Is it "slain" on the carpet? Is it tithing to the penny, or giving an offering *above* the tithe?

Is *this* what it must *do* to produce much fruit?!

No…it is resting.

We are not fruit producers through our amazing efforts. We are abiding. Abide means live. All we have to do is wake up each day and relax, and live our lives.

"No way, Matt! You're just saying people can be lazy! You will answer for these lies!"

Friend, is Christ lazy? I would say no. Who are we resting in?…*Him*.

Yes, it is a strange paradox, but once I began to understand this truth—that if I felt *pressured* it was not coming from God—everything changed. And to be honest with you, I "produce" more now than I ever have in my life. Why? Because I'm doing it from a state of rest. I'm not simply trusting Jesus for my one-time forgiveness, but for His minute-by-minute guidance.

God wants to do the same for you. He really does. If you're tired of the religious hamster wheel, if you've given it your best shot but you still *feel* like there's more—rest. *Strive* to rest. Strive. To. Rest.

Realize you are a branch. What does a branch do or not do? Friend, branches just *be*. Christians just *be*.

So how do you know if you're truly resting? How do you know if you're truly *being*? As a branch, this is the fruit of the Spirit of Christ—the vine—which will be produced through your actions and attitudes without effort:

"love, joy, peace, patience, kindness, goodness, faithfulness, gentleness, self-control" (See Galatians 5:22,23)

So today, my friends, know this: Try your very hardest to rest. Just try. As you do, you'll be *trusting* Jesus. I've never known anyone who has understood this truth and gone buck wild in sin—as a matter of fact, just the opposite. I've witnessed someone who finally realized that sin has no part of them as a branch, and that sin will never come from the vine they're connected to. In turn, fruit of the Spirit grew in truckloads from this person. That person is me. This is why I *know* that once *you* finally grasp who you truly are, Christian, the same fruit will fall from you, all over the place. So just be yourself. You have all you need for a restful, productive life.

A prayer for you: *Heavenly Father, thank you for opening up my eyes to who I am, your child. As your child, you never pressure me to be myself. Instead, you encourage me, counsel me, love me, lift me up and guide me into who I really am. Thank you for being such a good Father. Right now, I lift up all who are reading this, directly to you. For those who have been working so very hard for you, let them know they don't have to work hard. They just need to rest. Let them know you are completely satisfied with them. Because of their faith in the Cross, this satisfaction of yours is on a level in which they cannot comprehend. Even if they never do another thing for you for the rest of their lives, you're still infinitely proud of them. Teach them balance, Dad. Teach them authenticity. Let them know about the power that comes from within, Jesus, as they live their lives in Him. Amen.*

Day 10

Go and Sin No More?

Then Jesus straightened up and asked her,
"Woman, where are your accusers? Has no
one condemned you?" "No one, Lord," she
answered. "Then neither do I condemn you,"
Jesus declared. "Now go and sin no more."

John 8:10,11

"We should kill her! We should *kill* this nasty Jezebel!" The mob yells loudly, throwing a woman caught in the act of adultery at the feet of Messiah.

"What do you think Jesus?! Moses commanded us to stone someone such as this!"

Christ, stooped to the ground, begins writing in the dirt with His finger. Knowing they wanted to trap Him based on the Law, He does not give an answer right away.

"TELL US! What would *you* do to this woman?!"

In the dry soil, I can picture Jesus writing the words *mercy* and *grace*, because according to the Law of Moses–which could not be chopped up–this woman rightfully deserved to be executed. Some claim that Jesus was writing the names of each accuser, based on this Old Testament Scripture from Jeremiah 17:13:

> "LORD, you are the hope of Israel; all who forsake you will be put to shame. <u>Those who turn away from you will be written in the dust</u> because they have forsaken the LORD, the spring of living water."

Either way, peeking up from His writing, He replied, "Whoever is without sin, cast the first stone at her" (see John 8:7). Sin according to *what*? The Mosaic Law. This wasn't sin according to the preacher who is sweating profusely while running around like a madman trying to get the world to, "Stop all that sinnin'!"

No. This was sin, according to the Law.

This wasn't sin according to the Betty Blue-Hairs who don't like that "fast worship singin'," or them short-pants and messy hairdos worn by "those kids" in the house of God. "How dare they do such a thing, Edith! Sinful disrespect, I tell ya! I feel sorry for them on their Day of Judgment!"

No. This was sin, *infractions*, according to the Law for the Jews. None of us Gentiles were included, even if we're claiming to know *exactly* what sin is.

So when Jesus said, "Fire away if you've not sinned," the Jewish people looked at one another with a guilty frown. All of them knew they were failing horrendously at following *everything* Moses commanded in the Law–which is required–so they dropped their rocks and walked away.

Jesus then stood up and looked forward. With compassion He asked the woman, "Where are your accusers? Has no one condemned you?" (John 8:10).

Again, accusers of what? Condemned according to *what*? The Mosaic Law. 613 commandments which included the Ten Commandments. One of those 613, the act of adultery, required both parties to be killed:

"If a man commits adultery with another man's wife—with the wife of his neighbor—both the adulterer and the adulteress are to be put to death."
(Leviticus 20:10)

This wasn't even the "Thou shalt not commit adultery" commandment. This was, "You're *dead* if you get caught cheating." And where was the man whom she was cheating with? According to the Law, he would need to be killed as well. Was he one of the Pharisees in the crowd, cloaked with a stone in hand acting religiously innocent? We can only guess because it's not written, but it takes *two* people to commit adultery and only the *woman* was being accused of breaking this law.

"No one, Lord," she said to Jesus, after He asked her who's condemning her.

"Then neither do I condemn you. Now go and sin no more" (see John 8:11).

"See Matt! *GO AND SIN NO MORE!*" a grace-confused person belts away at me for teaching this passage according to the New Covenant. "You're just being easy on sin! Even Jesus said it right *there*, go and sin no more!"

Isn't it a peculiar thing how we get infuriated when what we define ourselves by is threatened? For this person barking at me, they're finding their identity in how *they* supposedly "go and sin no more." But are they *really* going and sinning no more? No. No they are not. And if they say they *are*, they're not telling the truth, therefore compounding their inability to go and sin no more. Do you see the hypocrisy?

This is the same reason the mob dropped their rocks and went home. They all knew they still sinned.

Unfortunately, many Christians today have a death-grip on sin-stones, one in each hand. They're ready to pummel the first person they see who is caught in a failure, mistake, addiction, or mishap. They claim that *I* am being lax on sin, but who's really doing so? My message–*it's impossible to go and sin no more based on the Law,* which is the proper context–holds the standard of the Law in high esteem. Yet they are saying it *is* possible to go and sin no more, based on the Law, but can't achieve this status themselves.

The Jews who were quick to walk away from the potential killing of this woman did so because they *knew* the Law required absolute perfection. If you fail at one of the 613 laws, you fail at all of them. This included the moral laws:

> *"Do not <u>add to</u> what I command you and <u>do not subtract from it</u>, but <u>keep the commands</u> of the Lord your God that I give you."*
> *(Deuteronomy 4:2)*

Growing up, I was taught that the Ten Commandments were the standard for Christians. This is wrong. What makes us think we only have to follow ten? The truth is, the Ten Commandments were only ten of the 613 commandments given to Israel from Moses after he brought them out of slavery from Egypt. And as you can see in the verse above, you can't *add* to it, nor take away from it. Plus, we aren't Jewish, so we were never even invited *to* obey the 613– let alone the Ten Commandments. If we tried, they'd laugh at us Gentiles and walk away saying, "Ha! *We* are God's chosen people, not you! Heathens!"

If you do a quick Google search for "What are the 613 commandments in the Mosaic Law" you'll be bored to tears before you even get halfway through reading them. Yet *we*, as non-Jews, like to pick out *just* ten–or nine plus tithing. So who's really being light on sin? It's the cherry-pickers of the Law. Modern legalists who couldn't hold a candle to the "righteousness" of the Pharisees, yet believe they're better than other Christians because of what they do and don't do. It's those who like to add to and subtract from 613 laws to their liking, then get mad at every person who doesn't "obey" like them. Come *off* of it.

Friend, not only were we *not* invited to obey the Law, if we *were,* as Christ taught, perfection is the standard. Jesus emphasized this to the Jews in the Sermon on the Mount (see Matthew 5:48). James reiterates the measure to his Law-loving buddies who wouldn't turn to faith in Christ, and Paul harps on the Mosaic perfection *required* to the Galatians who wanted to add Law in with the gospel. Here's what they said:

> *"For whoever keeps the whole law and yet stumbles at <u>just one point</u> is guilty of breaking all of it." (James 2:10)*

> *For all who rely on the works of the law are under a curse, as it is written: "Cursed is everyone who does not <u>continue to do everything</u> written in the Book of the Law." (Galatians 3:10)*

"What are you saying, Matt?! That it's okay to just go out and commit adultery?! Are you saying this woman didn't need to stop her sinning?!"

No. My friend, that's not what I'm saying. Adultery harms countless families in many ways. *Please* turn from it. Stop. Repent. Do a 180. Turning from adultery is a very healthy thing to do because there's no life in it. We weren't *made* for it. Like God, we were made to enjoy covenants and commitment.

Physical and emotional adultery only causes pain for everyone involved, *this* is why Jesus said, "Go and sin no more." It's because He didn't want this woman to be ensnared in the trap she just got out of. It's good to go and *not* have sinful actions and attitudes, but this is not a *commandment* by Christ.

Remember, anytime Jesus gave a legalistic commandment He was setting that person up for failure so they'd lean toward faith in Him alone. If He gave an impossible-to-do task it was for that reason–because with man it *would be* impossible, but through *Him,* nothing would be impossible (see Matthew 19:26, Philippians 4:12,13).

The rich young ruler was told to sell everything when he asked Jesus a Law-based question on how to inherit eternal life. So Jesus not only gave him a Law-based answer but He added even *more* impossible tasks on *top* of the commandments in the Law to show the young man he needed a better way *other* than self-effort. He loved him enough to teach him that righteousness would never be found in his non-sinning choices. Many preachers today will use this parable as a way to hound their congregations to "Give until it hurts!" but this is *not* a "Be generous with your money if you want to go to heaven" passage. This was a teaching on legalistic, *Mosaic* pride (see Mark 10:17-27, Matthew 19:16-26).

After all, according to the Old Covenant, if you *were* rich you were seen as a righteous person because God blessed the Law-keepers with great wealth. Those who meditated on His commandments day and night, were prosperous (see Joshua 1:8, Psalm 1:2). This is why the disciples were bamboozled when Jesus said it's easier for a camel to fit through the eye of a needle than for a rich man to make it to heaven. Such a statement went against everything they had been taught about wealth equaling righteousness (see Proverbs 15:6, Matthew 13:12, 19:23-25, 25:29).

The Sermon on the Mount, in Matthew 5, was the same. Jesus wasn't speaking in hyperbole when He said "cut off your hand, pluck out your eye, be perfect like God." Oh no. He was upping the standard of the Law of Moses for those who believed they were actually doing it. This is not a sweet teaching of "try your hardest" for Christians. This was a death sentence for the Jews who looked to the Law for righteousness. Repeatedly, He said, "You have heard *this*" and "You have heard *that*," well what was it they had heard? THE LAW OF MOSES. *His* commandments. *His* laws. Not Jesus'. Why do you think they wanted to kill Him? He was unraveling their religious identity. That's why.

The Sermon on the Mount wasn't directed at believers, but blasphemers (see Mark 3:28-30). Those who refused to accept the Spirit of Christ into their own *as* their righteousness. For this reason, Jesus said He didn't come to abolish the Law or the foretellings of the Prophets, but instead to reveal the true standard: perfection or bust!

> *"Do not think that I have come to abolish the Law or the Prophets; I have not come to abolish them but to fulfill them. For truly I tell you, until heaven and earth disappear, not the smallest letter, not the least stroke of a pen, will by any means disappear from the Law until everything is accomplished. Therefore anyone who sets aside one of the least of these commands and teaches others accordingly will be called least in the kingdom of heaven, but whoever practices and teaches these commands will be called great in the kingdom of heaven." (Matthew 5:17-19)*

Every single person listening to Him *was* setting aside commandments, that's why He said this. Therefore, *none* of them would be called great in the kingdom of heaven. Even the most devout Pharisees, such as Paul when he still went by Saul, would be sent to hell! (See Philippians 3:4-9, Acts 7:54-60, 8:1, Luke 13:27,28).

For those soaking up this sermon—just the same as the people who walked away from stoning the adulteress—everyone loosened their top button, gulped deeply and said, "I need you to save me, Messiah! I can't do this!" That, or they yelled out, "Let's crucify Him!"

What was Jesus doing? He was exposing their religious, sin-focused hypocrisy! As His Spirit does for us today, He was teaching them they *couldn't* do all the Law required! They needed a better way!

Him!

Grace!

A new, righteous spirit led by His Spirit *in* them!

The same spiritual relationship Adam and Eve had with God before the first sin! ONENESS! He was letting them know they had to be born again by faith in *His* forgiveness *from* their Law-breaking! (See John 1:12, 3:6,7,16,17, 14:6, Ephesians 2:8,9, Colossians 1:22, 3:3, 1 Corinthians 6:17,19).

So today, my friends, know this: When Jesus said, "Go and sin no more," this was not a commandment. It was loving advice for a person who believed that sin would make them happy. It wouldn't. Jesus knew that. Going and sinning no more is a *very* burdensome commandment–as was the entire Book of the Law. But Jesus' two *new* commandments, *apart* from the Mosaic Law, were not burdensome: *believe in Him and love as He has loved us* (see 1 John 3:23, 5:3, John 13:34, Romans 7:8).

Do this, and you'll sin no more, a whole lot more.

A prayer for you: *Father, today I want to thank you for opening up my eyes to the true meaning of Jesus' legalistic teachings. All along, it was meant to shut the mouths of every person who thought they were Law-abiding citizens–your Word says so in Romans 3:19. For years, as I read these passages I shuddered. But your Spirit has revealed to me that there's no fear in your love. Instead, your love casts out all fear. 1 John 4:18 tells me that fear has to do with punishment, and you will never punish me for not obeying a single commandment given by Moses. Jesus' commandments are better! I'm dead to all laws and alive in Christ! Thank you! Right now, I lift up all who are reading this, directly to you. So many of them*

are confused, Dad. They've been taught a mixture of Law and grace, and Jesus said doing so is the same as putting new wine into old wineskins—the wineskin will burst. Mark recorded these words in his Gospel, Mark 2:22, so I know it's the truth. This happens when we mix Jesus' impossible teachings in with our New Covenant message. The Jews couldn't even do this stuff so what makes us think we can? The Law was never meant to be a part of our lives! Instead, Christ is our life! Take us deeper, Father! Reveal that sinning no more was only accomplished by your Son, from birth to death, and now He lives inside of us! What an amazing free gift of sinless righteousness! In His name, I pray, amen.

Day 11

You Don't Have Two Selves

*"For we know that our old self was crucified with him
so that the body ruled by sin might be done away
with, that we should no longer be slaves to sin–because
anyone who has died has been set free from sin."*

Romans 6:6,7

For a moment, just imagine it. The Father witnessed Jesus dying on the Cross, and He speaks:

"Sin has been punished in full! I can finally join each and every person on earth *in* their spirit! I can now remove their sinful hearts and replace it with *my* heart! All they must do is believe my Son has forgiven them, and we can become one! But, I'm still going to make sure part of them is sinful. They need to have a sinful self to fight each day. After all, I don't want them to go wild with this grace! There must be a balance! Too much confidence in what Jesus has just done would be a bad thing. I'll join them, but only the *good* part. The perfectly-cleansed-forever section of their being? Yes. But the sinful side? Nope. They're on their own. That side—I'll call it their *bad self*—can cause me to go back on this promise I just made to my Son. They need to deny this part of their nature! Their bad self will have to battle it out with their good self until they die!"

...What a cruel, cruel god. What a *lying* god. Of course, this isn't the real God, but a description of a double-talking, two-timing deity, religion has made up. Certain churches need a way to explain why we still sin—even though we're forgiven—and what to do about it. "Deny your sinful self!"

The facts are this:

1. *Christians still sin, a lot, and all sins are deliberate.*
2. *Christians don't have a sinful self, we only have a sinless self.*

The problem is, when we don't understand the difference in our spirit, soul, and body—and what the power of sin is—we can't rightfully divide God's truths. In desperation, we begin making stuff up to suit our flavor of churchianity, having a full repertoire of twisted excuses. Non-gospel, error-filled jargon in which we *think* that if we're super-smooth or super-aggressive, will be believable.

The idea that we Christians are in a civil war with ourselves until we die—feeding the good dog within, and starving the bad dog—is hocus pocus. We're not fighting a war, and we don't *have* a bad dog. If we did, then Christ would not be able to make His home in us and the Cross wasn't so great.

Jesus said a house divided will fall (see Mark 3:25). When the religious people were making the claim that He was driving out demons by way of demonic power, Christ made clear that if He was full of demons, He'd leave the demons *in* people and *not* drive them out. "How can Satan drive out Satan?" He explained (see Mark 3:23).

Same with us today. How can Christ drive out Christ? Believer, *you* house Christ! In your body, Jesus lives there! In your spirit, He resides! (See 1 John 4:13, 1 Corinthians 6:17,19).

"I get that, Matt. But He still wants me to crucify my flesh! My flesh is extremely sinful!"

Friend, your flesh isn't sinful, it's holy. It was God's idea! And if you crucified it—which would be impossible after the first nail—you'd be pushing up daisies. Your body is but a tool for your spirit to use. It's an apparatus. Yes, your spirit was crucified, but not your body, not your flesh. Your spirit, soul, *and* body are blameless! (See 1 Thessalonians 5:23).

However, there are certain passages in the Bible where it seems as if our body is running amuck. The word *flesh* is used, and appears to be evil. But *flesh* doesn't always mean *body*. Sometimes it means the power of sin *through* the body—as a conduit. There's nothing wrong with the tube—our body—it's what's passing *through* it—sin. Our flesh by itself is just fine.

The power of sin is but an invisible smog covering every inch of planet earth. *It* can do nothing on its own and needs a host. Our flesh is that host. Sin can even influence our physical brains—therefore giving us sinful thoughts—then it *accuses* us that those thoughts *describe* us. But they do not. This is why you can be in a room by yourself, perfectly still, not watching or listening to anything, and a sinful *idea* hit you. That was sin. That was not *you*, Christian, but the force, the power of sin.

Although demons can pester us—but not touch us (see 1 John 5:18)—dark forces aren't always the culprits chattering away, telling us bad stuff. Instead, the force of sin *on* our brain is to blame.

Sinful thoughts can even be religious thoughts. Jesus told a parable about a well-behaved religious man acting "in the flesh" and a humble man acting according to humility—which is what God is looking for:

To some who were confident of their own righteousness and looked down on everyone else, Jesus told this parable: "Two men went up to the temple to pray, one a Pharisee and the other a tax collector. The Pharisee stood by himself and prayed: 'God, I thank you that I am not like other people— robbers, evildoers, adulterers—or even like this tax collector. I fast twice a week and give a tenth of all I get.'

But the tax collector stood at a distance. He would not even look up to heaven, but beat his breast and said, 'God, have mercy on me, a sinner.'

I tell you that this man, rather than the other, went home justified before God. For all those who exalt themselves will be humbled, and those who humble themselves will be exalted." (Luke 18:9-14)

The Pharisee was walking according to the flesh–exalting himself by way of Mosaic Law observance. Even though he appeared to be holy by religious standards, he was acting *out* sin through his physical members: hands, feet, brain, and *mouth*. The tax collector, however, knew he was living a messed up life and needed God's help. Keep in mind, this was pre-Cross and Old Covenant, this man was *not* saved because Christians are not sinners, but saints. Afterwards, through this profession by way of faith in Christ, he *would* have become a saint! (See Ephesians 4:12, Romans 1:7, 1 Corinthians 1:2, Colossians 1:2).

But truthfully, the tax collector could have easily acted like the Pharisee– confident in his sinful actions and attitudes. That would be walking according to the flesh as well. There's religious flesh and non-religious flesh, both are sin *through* the body. Even thoughts created through our brain such as jealously– *inward* flesh–is sin infiltrating our earth-pod.

Therefore, *the flesh* is not always our body by itself. Our body, by itself, is a suit for our spirit to walk around on this planet. It is good. *The flesh* is the power of sin coming to life through the body. Sin–not the verbs of *sinning* but the force like gravity–entered this realm when Adam and Eve first chose to disobey God. So the flesh mentioned quite often in the Bible, more often than not, is referring to sin through our body (see Romans 5:12, Genesis 4:7, James 1:15, Galatians 5:16-23).

You'd think the power of sin would be snuffed out through more behavior-focused, "Repent!" sermons, but just opposite! Sin is *enhanced* by Mosaic Law pressure, the Ten Commandments, and modern-day church rules! When the thou shalts come barreling at sin, it gets stirred up and agitated! It explodes with full force! (See Romans 5:20, 7:5-17).

But–that is *sin* and *not* us. We are separate.

Now that I've established what sin is, let's break down our human, three-part makeup. Understanding this changed everything for me! We are:

1. **Spirit.** The everlasting part of you. The real you. Your identity. Your spirit is ether 100% sinful or 100% holy. There is no middle ground based on what we do or don't do. This is your authentic self. For Christians, this is the self Paul describes in Romans 6–the self which was crucified with Christ–killed off. DEAD. That *old* self was naturally *full* of the power of sin. That spirit had to die *so that* Christ could join our new, sinless spirit. God isn't trying to get unbelievers to "clean up their lives" as some might think. No, He's trying to kill them. Once we allow Him to kill off our sinful spirit, by grace through faith in the Cross, He gives us a new self. A perfect self. A holy, blameless, sanctified in full self! A spirit who is *currently* enjoying heaven with Jesus! (See Romans 6:6,7, Hebrews 10:10,14, Colossians 1:22, 3:3, 2 Corinthians 5:17, Galatians 2:20, Ephesians 2:6).

2. **Soul.** The customizable part of you. Some people call it the conscience. It can be trained by the power of sin, Satan, demons, this

world–*or* by the Holy Spirit. Your soul is your mind, free will, and emotions. It is your thinker, chooser, and feeler. It's not holy or unholy, sinful or sinless. It is the *description* of your actions and attitudes at any given time. Your soul matures or digresses in maturity. It's educated by what and *who* you are allowing it to be influenced by. For this reason, we must protect it. Your eyes, ears, hands and feet, all lead to your soul–not your spirit–which is sealed up inside of God. Your spirit can't be touched, your soul *can* be shaped. Guarding what we regularly watch and listen to, from ungraceful garbage and things of this world, matters. Legalistic teaching and attending sin-rampant places can't change our identity, but such can weaken our soul. As a Christian, our soul is meant to be led by our spirit, who is combined with *the* Spirit! (See Romans 12:2, Philippians 1:6, 4:8, 1 Peter 5:7, 2 Peter 1:5-9, Ephesians 1:13, 1 John 5:18).

3. **Body.** The shell your spirit uses to walk this planet as a part of physical matter. A tool. An instrument. A vehicle. It can be used *by* our holy spirit for good things, or it can be *influenced* by the power of sin–resulting in walking according to the flesh and producing bad fruit. The Holy Spirit is in a constant battle with the flesh, *it* is attempting to prevent *you* from doing the good things which come naturally from your spirit. The flesh–sinful actions and attitudes *through* the body, even the brain–is what the Spirit is fighting. The Spirit is not fighting *us* or a bad version of our *self*. We are not "the flesh"–we are separate. Remember that. We are a blameless spirit who was reborn *in* Christ's Spirit, who has a soul, which is expressed through our body. When the Spirit is at war with the flesh (sin through our body) it's *our* job to take a step back, *stop* fighting, and *start* trusting Him to do His work. When we relax, we *don't* fight sin and the Spirit overpowers the flesh, not us. *They* are at battle with

one another, not *us*. As we walk according to our true selves–our spirit combined with *the* Spirit–our body produces good spiritual fruit! (See John 1:12, 3:6,7, 15:5, Galatians 5:16-24, 1 Corinthians 6:17, Ephesians 2:10).

As you can see, we don't have two selves. We have one self, a good self! ALL OF US IS GOOD! We don't have two natures. We have one nature–God's nature! (See 2 Peter 1:4).

"But Matt, my Bible says I have a sinful nature."

That was a mistake by the publisher. In order to be more readable, the words *sinful nature* were substituted for *flesh* in the 1984 version of the NIV Bible. Since then, they've changed it back to flesh. Why? Because the original Greek word was *sarx* which means *flesh*. It doesn't mean sinful and it doesn't mean nature. It means *flesh*. So when we read our Bibles, we need to look at each instance of flesh and determine whether or not the context is our body, or sin *through* the body.

The confusion of sinful nature replacing flesh has messed up a lot of people's theology–mine included, for quite some time. But think about it, if Christians are *naturally* sinful, then what better a reason to continue sinning? I mean, it's just a natural thing to do, right? This is why Satan wants you to believe you *do* have a sinful nature.

When we understand that we aren't naturally sinful–that we are sinless spirits with a physical body which can be influenced by a separate force *called* sin–we can start to walk according to *who* we know we are! We are God's children! We are good people with good hearts! Sin is *not* us–it's a parasite–something *in* us but *not* us. It's something we can act *out* but never become, because we've been supernaturally reborn *sinless* (see 1 John 3:9).

The power of sin in the original Greek is *hamartia*. That is your enemy, and the Spirit fights it, not you. Your body is not your enemy and your *self* is not your enemy. Demonic forces use this power to make you think something's wrong with you. But in fact, they know everything is *right* with you! Christian, you are just as righteous as Jesus Christ! (See 2 Corinthians 5:21, 1 John 4:17).

So today, my friends, know this: Believer, you have one self, a self whom God is well pleased! You don't need to deny yourself, but *be* yourself! As you do, sin stands no chance! When Jesus said you must deny yourself in Matthew 16, He was rebuking Peter who just told Him to *not* go to the Cross. As a matter of fact, Jesus called him Satan. Ouch. But Jesus was aware of who was behind such a thought–the devil, not Peter. God doesn't want Christians to deny who we are, why would He want such a thing? After all, Jesus gave us His life so we could have life–*His* life! So be yourself today!

A prayer for you: *Father, thank you for revealing to me that I have a self just like you. Through the New Covenant, I've inherited your very Spirit combined with my spirit–giving me a heavenly self. Keep teaching me more about who you've made me to be, and empower me to walk it out. Right now, I lift up all who are reading this, directly to you. So many of them are confused. They've been taught they need to feed their good self and starve their bad self–but that's wrong according to your Word. They simply need to live OUT their good self, and realize they don't HAVE a bad self. The power of sin can influence their flesh and mind–but THEY aren't sinful at all. Take us deeper into the knowledge of this truth, and the grace in which we've tapped into it. In Christ's name I pray, amen.*

Day 12

Is "Once Saved Always Saved" True?

"What must I do to be saved?"

See Acts 16:30

Once Saved Always Saved is a touchy subject for those who don't understand what Christ has fully done *for* us and *to* us. To prove that Once Saved Always Saved is true, I need to first build on what saves and what doesn't.

I was recently scrolling through social media and I read a post about a near-death experience. This person had been in a drowning accident and died in the water. Miraculously, she was revived after being pulled onto a boat; yet she still spent quite some time with no pulse. She was dead.

Her post was her testimony, and testimonies are always amazing to hear or read. I loved it.

However, she said that as she drifted away, all she could feel was shame because her life had "shown no evidence of belief in Him." Was she already saved? I don't know, but evidence of belief doesn't save us, only the actual *belief* does. If evidence saved us, how can we be sure we've got enough of it? Where is the finish-line tape of evidence that we break through of being *absolutely, positively, 100%* sure?

Sadly, if we have a definitive answer we are placing our faith in ourselves. And even *more* sad, if we answer that question with a non-definitive answer– yet we still believe it's evidence that saves us–we will live in fear. Faith in what we do or don't do, as evidence, is not proof of faith. Faith is the substance of things *not* seen (see Hebrews 11:1).

This person went on to type, "Nothing we can do can save our soul except accepting His grace." So which is it? Is it the evidence–as she previously said–or is it grace, as she just finished up her post with? It can't be both. Paul explains:

> *"And if by grace, then it <u>cannot be based on works</u>; if it were, <u>grace would no longer be grace</u>." (Romans 11:6)*

Why would I reference this verse? Because evidence is created *through* works–or gifts. I'm not going to go over gifts in this devotional (you can search my past devotionals to find more on that subject). But even when we *express* our gifts, this only happens organically by way of expressing Christ *without* effort.

Anyway, back to the matter at hand: evidence of faith by works.

Another verse might come to mind, from the book of James:

> *"So also faith by itself, if it does not have works, is dead." (James 2:17)*

Now, in context, James is writing to his unbelieving Jewish friends. Anytime the Old Testament is mentioned as "ground to stand on" the Jews are in focus–not us stinky Gentiles. This passage is a plea for them to place their faith in Christ–in full. By using the examples of *two* separate people who expressed a *one-time* action of faith–Rahab and Abraham–Jesus' brother builds his case for *expressing* faith in Christ *through* action.

The readers of this letter were bent on believing *their* Scripture, so James gives them two examples of people *from* their Scripture who had expressed their faith through one-time actions. It wasn't the actions in themselves that justified their faith but the faith behind their single action.

The truth is, Rahab, who was a non-Jew prostitute, *believed* God and helped out the Jewish spies. It wasn't the *action*, but the faith *behind* it that mattered. James doesn't say, "She was a fellow Israelite"–which she *had* to be if she wanted to be righteous by *their* Law. Nor does he say she stopped prostituting and lived a righteously behaved life. Instead, his focus was her one-time action *backed up by faith*–an action which would never have happened if she did not *first* believe God.

He then uses the example of Abraham offering Issac on an altar. Again, it wasn't him placing his son on the platform that justified Abraham, but the faith *behind* it (see James 2:21-26). Abraham was already credited as righteous with God way before Issac was born, by faith alone (see Genesis 15:6, Romans 4:3).

Do you see it? Friend, it's not our evidence or *actions* that save us but the faith from within them! Again, Rahab wasn't even an Israelite–she was a Gentile–and this was *before* the New Covenant which was brought in by the Cross! Us Gentiles–all non-Jewish people–weren't even *allowed* to follow God's commandments! Therefore, she didn't have the opportunity to be *considered* as righteous by obedience, yet she was used as an example of perfect faith!

This proves that mankind has always been justified with God by faith alone, even during the period of Mosaic Law (see Galatians 2:16,21). So yes, faith without works *is* dead–faith must be the bedrock of all authentic work! But even deeper, works without *faith* is dead.

This brings us to the conclusion that Once Saved Always Saved is true! Why? Because faith cannot be measured by evidence, and it is our one-time faith alone that saves us! How does a single moment of faith in Christ's forgiveness save? Because it causes us to be birthed! It is *faith* that makes us *re*born in our spirit, and our supernatural birth is what truly saves! (See John 1:12, 3:6,7).

Let's look at it like this: If you have a baby and you're holding it in the hospital, it's swaddled and oh so cute. But the first thing you speak to your child is this, "I sure hope you live up to our family name. If you don't, you're no longer my baby. I'll turn away from you and I might consider you being my baby again *if* you prove yourself. However, if your actions and attitudes aren't *just* right, you're going back into the womb and being turned into a sperm and an egg. I'll undo your birth and I might re-do it if you straighten up. Then, if you keep falling short of who you really are, you will not exist anymore. You need to die to yourself each day so that you don't die to me. Mess up too much? Ha! I'll let you *try* to still be my child, but if you don't repent and confess regularly–you're definitely out. So you *better* stay in line and I *might* bless you and take care of you–but *only* if you have plenty evidence of being in my family and give me 10% of your income."

You'd be out of your mind. This is madness. Your child can never be unborn from you–no matter what they do. *We* can never be unborn from God no matter *what* we do–or don't do! Birth is not contingent on actions and attitudes!

Yet this is exactly what happens when a Christian is made to think they must have evidence of being a child of God–of being saved once. Friends, this is not okay. We should be teaching believers who God has recreated them to be! We should be nourishing the built-in love inside them! We should be giving them confidence in their heaven-ready lineage and strong supernatural DNA structure! We should be treating them according to who they really are, not by how they always act!

If you're still not convinced that Once Saved Always Saved is the same as Once Born Always Born, here's some biblical truths to help build up your blessed assurance even more:

1. **The New Covenant is based on a promise between the Father and Son–not you. You are simply a beneficiary to that will by faith.** According to the Old Covenant there was a big problem: *the fault of the people* (see Hebrews 8:8). What was their fault? Their inability to keep their promise to God. When Moses gave the Law, the Israelites said, "We will do all of it!" (See Exodus 19:8). Yet before the "ink was even dry"–or the stone tablets cooled off–the people were already breaking the very first commandment. There was nothing *wrong* with the Old Covenant in itself–it's actually perfect (see Romans 7:7). Like today's works-focused Christians who think they are "doing all of it"–which is required in the Covenant–the issue was Israel's inability to live up to their end of the bargain: *follow 613 laws–perfectly* (see Galatians 3:10, James 2:10). Because they couldn't, they were forced to sacrifice their best animals once a year to remind them of how badly they kept breaking their promises–or "sinning" (see Hebrews 10:3,4). So God made a *new* Covenant with Himself– the Father and the Son–rather than with the people! Israel was cut out of the equation! We Gentiles were never *in* the equation! (See Colossians 3:11, Galatians 3:28). Perfect blood is required to create a Covenant with God, so Christ shed His blood at the Cross (see Hebrews 9:15). When this happened, the Old Covenant became obsolete (see Hebrews 8:13)–there was no further need for it for all who believed in Jesus. So, 613 commandments given by Moses–which ten of those commandments were *the* Ten Commandments–were now as a pay-phone or floppy disk for Spirit-filled people (see 2 Corinthians

3). The Law was fulfilled *in* Christ and now righteousness came by faith to all who would believe! (See Romans Romans 5:1, 10:4). The New Covenant made a *new* way for us to simply *inherit* God's own righteousness by grace through faith alone! This faith causes us to be supernaturally born into God's own family! We have become beneficiaries rather than promise keepers! (See 2 Corinthians 5:21, Ephesians 1:5, 2:8,9, John 3:16-18, Hebrews 6:13-19).

2. **The only way a Christian can lose their salvation is if Jesus dies again.** Since it's only blood that forgives us–and our one-time faith in that perfect blood (see Hebrews 9:22, 10:10)–we never have to worry. As long as Jesus stays alive, we stay alive! (See Hebrews 7:25, John 14:19, Colossians 3:4). Christ isn't dying in heaven again and again for each sin we commit, "It is finished!" were His dying words for a reason! (See John 19:30). The author of Hebrews tells us Jesus isn't *working* to keep us forgiven either, He's resting (see Hebrews 1:3). He presented His blood *once* (see Hebrews 9:12). His final sacrifice at the Cross–to bring in the New Covenant–believe it or not it *actually* worked! Sure, just like the Israelites, we think we are "doing our part" but that's foolish talk. Death is required for every sin–not behavior and attitude repentance–and Jesus already died! (See Romans 6:23, 2 Corinthians 5:21). So since we *have* inherited Christ's own righteousness by faith, our job is to simply learn more about who we are–from His Spirit within *our* spirit–and then be ourselves! (See 1 Corinthians 6:17, Colossians 3:3, Romans 12:2, Philippians 1:6, John 14:16,26, Galatians 5:22,23).

3. **Hebrews 10:26 is not written to Christians.** This is a go-to verse for the grace-confused people. Like the first terrible promise keepers, we can easily start to view a *single* verse legalistically while missing the big picture of faith. Hebrews 10:26 states, *"If we deliberately*

keep on sinning after we have received the knowledge of the truth, no sacrifice for sins is left"–and yes, this is true–FOR THE JEWS WHO WERE SACRIFICING ANIMALS TO GET FORGIVENESS. The author is writing to the unbelieving Jews in this part of his message, hence the title, *Hebrews*. They heard the gospel from the best teachers! But still, they wanted to keep getting forgiveness once a year from animal blood on the Day of Atonement which was presented to God by the levitical priests at the temple. They heard about Jesus in great detail–they had knowledge of the truth–but did not believe. Read all around it and you'll see the context as the author reiterates the true punishment for those who broke Moses' Law–and now, for those who trample on faith in the Messiah alone. Like their ancestors who wouldn't enter the promised land to find rest, these Hebrew people wouldn't enter the promised rest of believing in Jesus (see Hebrews 4:11). If this part of the letter was written to Christians, then Jesus would need to die again–*for each sin we commit*. THAT AIN'T HAPPENING. This is *not* a license to sin, as the person who struggles with self-righteousness will spout. We don't need a license. We all sin plenty without one and God does not grade on a curve. He requires spiritual perfection! (See Matthew 5:48, John 3:6,7,16,17). Even more, all Christians sin deliberately–a lot. If we say we don't, then we're lying, therefore compounding our sinful actions and attitudes with lies. Just get over it. You're forgiven. If you sin, stop. But stopping won't make you any more forgiven than you already are. It will just cause you to walk *out* who you already are–a holy saint.

4. **Matthew 7:21 is not written to Christians.** In this passage, those who have a tendency of legalanity will quote something Jesus said in order to create fear in others–*or* to make their own religious works the

foundation of their faith: *"Not everyone who says to me, 'Lord, Lord,' will enter the kingdom of heaven, but the one who does the will of my Father."* In context, Jesus is rebuking the religious hypocrites as they bragged on their miracles performed and spiritual gifts used, to *prove* they know God. But–in John 6:40, Jesus said that His Father's will is to *believe* in His Son, which they did not. These Israelites were being informed that their amazing works won't be worth anything when they stand before God–*if* that's what they want to go with rather than knowing *Him.* Just look: *"And then will I declare to them, 'I never knew you; depart from me, you workers of lawlessness'"* (Matthew 7:23). Two things: 1. Jesus *never* knew them. This is not a Christian who lost their salvation for lack of works, but a person who looked to their works *for* salvation and not faith in Christ. 2. They were being held to the standard of the Law, that's why they practiced–as Christ said, "lawlessness"–*rather* than believe in Him alone! What law could cause a person to practice lawlessness, in context? The only Law the Jews had–Moses'! 613 commandments in which *we* are dead to as believers in Christ! (See Romans 7:4, 10:4, Galatians 2:19).

So today, my friends, know this: Once Saved Always Saved is the truth! We don't have the ability to unsave ourselves–to unborn ourselves! If we could, then each time we sinned, Jesus would have to go back in time, climb back on the Cross, take Himself down, become a baby, go back into Mary, go back into heaven, then re-do His birth, life, death, and resurrection all over again! Our incorrect choices and thoughts are not more powerful than His decision to forgive us once and for all time! We cannot maintain our heavenly lineage nor improve it, just the same as we cannot maintain our *human* lineage nor improve it! We are born! Birth is final! We are children of God who are forever saved into eternity!

A prayer for you: *Dad, thank you for teaching me that I'm a child of yours who's been born into your family for good. Paul told us in Romans 8, we have the right to call you "Abba" which means "Daddy." My, what an honor! Thank you for sending Jesus here to give us this gift of free righteousness! Right now, I lift up all who are reading this, directly to you. So many of them have been lied to about who they are as a new creation in Christ. Please begin to reveal the truth of Scripture about what you've done to them through their faith in Jesus! I pray that you open up the eyes of their mind to match the eyes of their heart, where you live. In Jesus' name I pray, give them confidence, Dad. Teach them to never be afraid. Amen.*

Day 13

We All Get Paid the Same

"Don't I have the right to do what I want with my own money? Or are you envious because I am generous?"

Matthew 20:15

"Mark Smith, step on up," God says sternly with a displeased frown. Another person has died and now stands before Him to be judged and receive their heavenly rewards.

"You only worked for *this* amount of payment," our Creator explains with an eye-roll, while pointing to a pile of treasure the size of a small stack of books.

"Not very good, Mark, but go ahead over there and claim your earnings, then I'll have an angel show you to the slums. Truthfully, you're lucky to even sneak on in, let alone get *those* rewards. Now get out of my sight."

"Betty Ann Baker, you're next. What you did was just *okay*, I guess. There's your pile of crowns and jewelry in the wheelbarrow. You could have done a lot more, so you'll spend eternity in middle-class. And Betty, by the way, you irk me. You irked me on planet earth, and even now—so much wasted talent that I gave you. If you *really* wanted to make me proud you would have done much more, you would have *used* what I left with you for more good things. I expected a greater return on my investment. Now be gone. I might stop by and see you now and again, I might not. It's whatever. Your whole *life* was just *whatever*, so that's what you'll get from me for eternity."

"Next…" an angel calls out to the crowd.

"William Graham!" God gasps! "What an absolute honor it is to see you in my presence! Hang on—*hang on*—I have to direct the dump trucks of treasures to lay at your feet!"

Beep…beep…beep… The fleet of tandem diesels are piled to overflowing as they back up and pour out what looks like a bigger booty than the contents of the bank from DuckTales! Confetti explodes everywhere! Celebratory music comes belting from the angels! The Father, Son, and Holy Spirit all run out to shake the hand of Reverend Billy Graham!

Gazing in adoration, the Trinity speaks together in one voice, "We have the greatest spot for you inside! Come on in and see! Oh we are so blessed to have you here! Finally! We're not sure what we would have done on that evil, *evil* planet without you! Come! Come see all of your rewards and the huge palace we've built with your name at the top of it!"

…With all due respect to Billy Graham, whom I love, just imagine if this was the truth. For a moment, picture God doling out levels of medals, merchandise, and mansions for all we've done and *not* done while living in these fragile shells. This is not how it works for Christians. We all get paid the same. Even the symbolic elders in Revelation 4:10 cast their crowns at the feet of Jesus. So what makes us believe *we* will be paid in measurements on Judgment Day?

"No way, Matt! Jesus said in Revelation 22:12 that when He comes back He'll repay us for the work we've done!"

Friend, that's true, but He also defines what *work* truly is for a Christian, in John 6:29:

"The work of God is this: to believe in the one he has sent."

The work is to believe. Also, in that same verse, Revelation 22:12, He said His reward is *with* Him! *He* is that reward! I understand this upsets the most self-righteous because I'm messing with their "stuff." After all, they've worked way too hard to not get paid (see Matthew 7:21-23). But at the same time, this truth is a life-giving relief for those who can't find rest, no matter how much work they do (see Matthew 11:28-30).

In the Parable of the Talents found in Matthew 25:14-30, Jesus talks about a master with three servants. Each one of them was entrusted with "talents" or "bags of gold." The master heads off on a trip, expecting each to invest their talents and get a return for him. Two of them do, one of them does not. The servants who *do* turn in their talents with interest, the master is greatly pleased with. The one who doesn't is scolded and cast out into the darkness where there is weeping and gnashing of teeth–which sounds like hell to me.

Now, I have some colleagues who see this parable as the talents being the gospel, and God rewarding us for what we do with it–and I respect that view. I've even used this example in my previous books. However, I believe an even *deeper* look into this passage is Jesus explaining what judgment is like under the Mosaic Law–with the ante' being upped. After all, no Christian will be given "more" gospel in heaven for investing in it on earth; and no Christian will be "cast out" for *not* investing in the gospel. We are God's children by birth and are not judged by anything we invest. Instead, we are judged by our lineage (see John 1:12, 3:6,7, 5:24).

This is why I see this passage as Mosaic Law Judgment 2.0. Remember, the Bible was not written in chapters and verses. Those were added later for easy referencing. So I see this parable as Christ saying, "If you want to be judged according to the talents God has given you, this is what you'll get. So you better get to work or else!"

Sounds scary to me! Yet God has not given me a spirit of fear, but of peace, confidence, love, and a sound mind (see 2 Timothy 1:7, Galatians 5:22,23). And if I'm looking at this parable as a goal of investing the gospel, how can I be sure I've invested well enough? Such a thought can send chills down my spine if I allow it–and I won't!

According to the book of 1 John, God's love for me is perfect and it casts out all fear because fear has to do with punishment. Christians won't be punished for anything by God because Christ was already punished. The only thing He *would* punish us for is sin, and *every* sin requires a death, and Jesus isn't dying over and over because of my "lack" of investing in the gospel based on my level of God-given talent (see Romans 6:23, Hebrews 1:3).

A child of God shouldn't be worried one iota about their Day of Judgment, we should be eagerly awaiting it! (See 1 John 4:17). So if I'm stressing about investing the gospel, how can I be eagerly awaiting judgment? I can't. Plus, this entire parable is based on a servant/master relationship, yet Christ said this:

> "I no longer call you servants, because a servant does not know his master's business. Instead, I have called you friends, for everything that I learned from my Father I have made known to you." (John 15:15)

Do we still *serve* God even though we are no longer His servants? Of course! But not out of fear–instead, out of love…out of delight. The New Covenant is based on a loving relationship, not a fearful one set upon expectations, duties, and punishment. God's expectations, duties, and punishment for me was put on Christ! Further, no true, *caring* union can ever be enjoyed through threats. So according to this parable, the people in it are *not* getting paid the same. Not even close. Jesus even said this toward the end:

"For whoever has will be given more, and they will have an abundance.
Whoever does not have, even what they have will be taken from them."
(Matthew 25:29)

That's not the gospel. The gospel isn't taken from us for not investing it. Nor is it given to those who have done more *to* invest it. This teaching from Jesus can be viewed as performance-based judgment, which is not how the New Covenant operates. Christ already performed everything *for* us. It is *His* talents that matter to the Father, not ours. We are branches, not investors.

On the other hand, the Parable of the Vineyard Workers is New Covenant judgment! In Matthew 20:1-16, Jesus explains that some labor is needed to be done in a vineyard, so the owner hires people to work. Each hired person agrees to work for the *same* set amount of wages—but all throughout the day the owner hires new laborers. Some started working at daybreak, others around lunch, and some didn't even begin until nearly the end of the workday.

Afterwards, when they all lined up to be paid, each received the exact same amount of payment. Those who started working early complained because of putting in more time, effort, and energy. Yet the owner retorts, "I can do whatever I want with my own money. What's it to you?"

He then says something which can be overlooked if we aren't paying close attention, an ending statement which is the *opposite* of the ending of the Parable of the Talents:

"So the last will be first, and the first will be last." (Matthew 20:16)

Do you see it?! We all get paid the same! This is not a Bible verse on pride, but on payment!

Sadly, so many of us have been taught we'll receive different levels of rewards in heaven based on our works or lack thereof. But what most believers don't know is that the word *rewards* (plural) is not in the New Testament, only *reward* is. And what's our reward? It's Christ in us, right now! It's a free gift of righteousness, today, permanently, in these finite human bodies! Just look!

> *"Do you not know that your bodies are temples of the Holy Spirit, who is in you, <u>whom you have received</u> from God?" (See 1 Corinthians 6:19)*

Our reward is the Holy Spirit of Christ! Paul tells the Romans:

> *"And if anyone does not have the Spirit of Christ, they do not belong to Christ." (See Romans 8:9)*

We *have* Him! We *belong* to Him! Even better, our reward, Christ in us, is *inherited* and not earned! Inheritances come by way of a death, and Christ died! Inheritances don't have the *possibility* of being earned! They are bequeathed! You can't tell your rich uncle that you'll work *really hard* for your portion of what he'll leave you—he has to die! Same with us and our righteousness from God! This is why the Jews who were waiting on Messiah were ecstatic! Those who were taught to *do, do, do,* could now rest, rest…*rest*… because of their inheritance from faith in the Cross of Christ.

Our full reward is the inheritance of Jesus' Spirit into our own. Paul informs the people in Colossae, as well as those in Corinth:

> *"knowing that from the Lord you will receive <u>the reward of the inheritance. It is the Lord Christ</u> whom you serve." (Colossians 3:24)*

"But whoever is united with the Lord is one with him in spirit."
(1 Corinthians 6:17)

This is *so* exciting to me! No wonder the gospel means good news! Friend, do you see that it is Christ whom you've inherited? *Now*? I am not talking about what you do, but who lives *in* you. As God's kids, we are not *waiting* to receive Jesus at the gates of heaven along *with* a bounty of gold coins and diamonds. No. Our reward–our *gift*–was given when we first believed: the Spirit of God, with a big, beautiful bow on top.

In heaven, the main thing that will happen is the complete removal of sin from our presence–a sinless realm–*that's* what heaven is! I'm not referring to the verbs of *sinning*–which is incorrect actions and attitudes for a saint. I'm talking about the *force* which entered this universe when Adam and Eve no longer believed God about their perfection by way of a *simple* relationship with Him (see Genesis 4:7, Romans 5:12). Sin is a force, a power like gravity. It's everywhere and affects everything, yet we cannot see it. *It* is what causes all death, decay, and destruction. *It* is the batter in which demonic forces use to cook up the most pain.

IN HEAVEN, THE POWER OF SIN WILL NOT BE THERE! Why do you think it's such a wonderful place?! Why do you think all tears will be wiped away?! It's because sin cannot be in God's presence so we will be taken *out* of it when we eject from these earth-suits! (See Revelation 21:4, 2 Corinthians 5:8).

As new creations *in* Christ, we are not waiting on heaven! We have heaven on the inside of us as we live and breathe today! IT IS JESUS! It is Jesus combined *with* our new, perfect spirits which we received the moment we first believed He forgave us! (See 1 Corinthians 6:17, Romans 6:6,7, 2 Corinthians 5:17, Galatians 2:20).

My goodness! I get so pumped up when I write about this subject! I even have to tell myself, "Now don't get too carried away," but the *fact* that Jesus lives in me in full as I type? ... That's incredible.

Yet some will still claim that it's *just* Jesus and *none* of me. That's not true. It's both of us together. It's a relationship. I am not a hollow tube, I'm a person. The Father isn't *only* looking at Jesus while saying, "Ewwww..." as He peaks over at me once in a while. *I* am righteous, *I* am holy, and *I* am blameless too! This is the gift for all who will believe! This is the reward we inherit by faith! What happened at the Cross, and our belief in it, sealed the deal of us becoming the beneficiaries *to* these heavenly traits! (See Colossians 1:22, 2 Corinthians 5:21, Ephesians 2:8,9, Romans 3:21,22, 11:6, Hebrews 9:15).

So today, my friends, know this: We've all been paid the same, as New Covenant believers! The reward is Christ in us right now! We aren't looking *forward* to being paid at heaven's door. Instead, we've *been* paid by grace through faith in Jesus' ability to perfect us *once* for all time–by one Sacrifice–Himself! (See Hebrews 10:10, 10:14). Your reward is Jesus living in you, *through* you, now and forevermore! Nothing else could ever compare!

A prayer for you: *Dad, thank you so much for the inheritance you've given me through the event which took place at the Cross. I feel so honored to even get to be here on this planet with your Spirit inside me. I have no words to describe how I feel about this, but you already know. Thank you. Right now, I lift up all who are reading this, directly to you. So many of them have been distracted by thinking they need to get to work to earn more stuff for when they die. Father, please renew their minds to the easiness of what Jesus has accomplished for them. Some have even been taught that there are two different judgments, and there's not. You are wise enough, and fair enough, to only need one. And yes, we must all appear before you to give an account for the good and bad done while in this body. But for*

Christians, we don't have anything bad, we only have good. Bad is sin, and Jesus has looked down the timeline of our life and taken those all away. You are satisfied with His death on the Cross for all of our sins committed. He was the one true propitiation. Therefore, the only thing that will be left on our Judgment Day–that hasn't burned up like wood, hay, and stubble–are the organic, good things we've done! Jesus said if we even do so much as give a cup of water in His name, we'll be rewarded! So we look forward to being judged! But even deeper, we already know that growing in your grace for all of eternity, through your Son, is the greatest reward we've ever received! In His name I pray, amen.

Day 14

How Can I Stop Worrying?

"Do not be anxious about anything, but in every situation, by prayer and petition, with thanksgiving, present your requests to God."

Philippians 4:6

Worry is a funny thing isn't it? Not funny "ha ha," but funny weird. You could be sitting on a park bench all by your lonesome with nothing happening–looking calm, cool, and collected–yet worry is flooding your mind like a raging waterfall. It's impossible to stop worrying 100%, but we can worry a lot less often when we recognize where it comes from: *fear.* Fear-filled thoughts of the *future.* We can even worry about something that's happened in the past, but is not yet complete.

Fear stems from three main things, none of which are from God:

1. The power of sin.
2. Demonic forces.

3. Old, unrenewed thoughts.

I want to go over all three in detail because if we can point out what the root cause of worry is, we can enjoy our lives even during the most strenuous circumstances–because we have nothing to fear. But first, let's look at Webster's definition of worry: to *think about* problems or fears : to *feel* or show fear and concern because you *think* that something bad has happened or *could* happen.

Ole' Webster was on to something, wasn't he?! Thinking about and feeling fear *causes* worry! Based on truth or not, thoughts and feelings can't always be controlled. As a part of our soul, they're like vapors. Our spirit is anchored in Christ, but our soul–mind, free will, and emotions–can easily flap like a flag in the wind. However, thoughts and feelings that cause worry *can* be directed and sorted into the proper bins. For this reason, Paul never told the early church, "You *better* feel different! You *better* have different thoughts!"

No. He gently advised them what to think about and what to focus on. Why? Because he knew if they would shift their minds onto the truth of Jesus–onto the truth of His grace and what He's done to them–only *then* would their thoughts and feelings shift as well. In turn, they'd be less worrisome and anxious, they'd be effective in infecting others with grace, and they'd enjoy their lives despite dire circumstances.

Paul understood that worrying would never change their identity, it would just make them shrink back and be quiet. So he encouraged them into *what* to think about. Look at this amazing advice:

> *"Finally, brothers and sisters, whatever is true, whatever is noble, whatever is right, whatever is pure, whatever is lovely, whatever is admirable–if anything is excellent or praiseworthy–think about such things." (Philippians 4:8)*

"Do not conform to the pattern of this world, but be transformed by the renewing of your mind." (See Romans 12:2)

"we take captive every thought to make it obedient to Christ" (See 2 Corinthians 10:5)

Thoughts lead to fear. Fear leads to feelings. Feelings lead to worry. Therefore, if we can corral the stuff in our mind with counsel from the Spirit, we can sift through *Truth and Lies, Controllable and Not Controllable.* Anxiety can then fade away.

When worry hits you, ask yourself a handful of questions to doubt your doubts:

"Has this happened yet? Is it going to? Do I have any control over this right now? Can I change the outcome while still living out my true self as a saint?"

All Christians are saints. Saint simply means holy, or set apart. Set apart from what? Sin. The world. That's exactly what happened to our spirit the moment we first believed (see John 1:12, 17:16, Ephesians 2:6, Romans 8:9-11, Hebrews 10:10,14).

Certain denominations have twisted this word *saint* by awarding it to individuals based on votes. Wrong. Every Christian is *equally* holy. Not by what we *do*, but by who we *are*. There's not a single verse in the New Testament where God, an apostle, or otherwise, awards sainthood to a particular person based on actions and attitudes. Instead, the Bible says we are *all* part of a royal priesthood! (See 1 Peter 2:9).

Since we have sanctified supernatural DNA as saints (sanctified also means holy), sometimes God wants to teach us the art of doing nothing at all.

Personally, this is one of the most difficult things I've ever had to learn. My old, unrenewed thoughts loved to worry when I wasn't actively trying to solve a problem. Just like Jesus telling the waves, "Peace! Be still!" my spirit was learning to do the same (see Mark 4:39).

Other times God is coaching us into how to conduct respectful confrontations, and how to establish healthy boundaries. You are *not* a punching bag. You are valuable. You shouldn't have to worry about being "less than" because you're standing up to unacceptable behavior. God wants you to help others but He doesn't want you to be responsible for them. Just look at the Good Samaritan. He helped the man who was hurt, but still went about his own business. He didn't stop his trip and coddle the injured fellow, hanging out at the inn, neglecting responsibilities. Not at all. He helped because he wanted to, and then moved forward with his own life (see Luke 10:25-37).

Religious manipulation will teach you the *opposite* of this. Don't fall for it. Be *confident*. Even if you're stammering, shaking, or stuttering, the Holy Spirit will empower you to stand up to fake spiritual extortion from a church. Not all churches are like this, but some are. Don't be afraid. Don't worry. Be you. You are loving, you are respectful, and you are holy. Help if you want. Don't help if you don't want. Your identity remains the same.

The ability to discern such things is fueled by God's grace *not* by self-made efforts. Remember, we are branches, He is the vine (see John 15:5, 2 Corinthians 12:9). The vine never stresses the branch out or tells it to worry. Nor does the vine ever guilt the branch into producing fruit.

My friend, worry comes from dreading the future. Most of the stuff we worry about *in* the future, never even happens. But if it does, we know who holds our future, we know who isn't bound by our human sense of time, Jesus (see 2 Peter 3:8, Revelation 22:13, Deuteronomy 31:8). If we look even deeper into the sovereignty of our Creator, when we rightfully deserve a bad outcome, we can still find rest in our minds and enjoy our lives because we know He is infinitely merciful. Just look at how He blessed Ismael, who was the result of Abraham attempting to rush God (see Genesis 17:20).

If you'll begin to question the questions of worry in your head, the Holy Spirit will give you the correct answers; answers which will lead you into peace, hope, confidence, and a sound mind! Let's look at the three things which can attempt to steer our thought life into the ditch:

1. **The power of sin.** Sin is a force on this planet which affects absolutely everything. Like gravity, you can't see it but it's *still* real. Not to be confused with the verbs of *sinning*, but the original Greek word, which is a noun, *hamartia*. The power of hamartia was not here when God created this universe. Our original ancestors' rebellion caused it to enter this physical realm. It is this force which makes everything eventually die. *It* causes pain, *it* causes sorrow, and *it* causes suffering–not God. God is good. Sin is the true culprit of *why* this planet is fallen. When bad things happen, if humanity would begin blaming sin, rather than our Creator, we'd be on the right track. Sin influences our minds *away* from the guidance of God's Spirit. Not us, but our thoughts. This causes extreme worry. Thankfully, as Christians, our spirit is brand new and sealed up in the sin-free realm–heaven–*as* you read this! Pay attention because this force even attempts to make you think *you* are sinful, believer. You're not. You're just as holy, righteous, and blameless as Jesus Christ! (See Genesis 4:7, Romans 5:12, 6:6-10, 2 Corinthians 5:21, 15:21,22, Galatians 2:20, 5:16-23, Ephesians 1:13, 2:6, 1 John 4:17)

2. **Demonic forces.** For years, before I understood the power of sin, I blamed everything on the devil and his demons, especially my worry-filled thoughts. However, demonic forces can't read brainwaves. They are individual troublemakers who like to work together in a group.

They can't get at God, so they'll attempt to get at who He loves, which is us. They pay close attention to our lives, noticing our weak spots and attacking them. They study how sin is influencing us—even from the time of our birth—then *tempting* us with such sinful tendencies. Are they clever? Yes. Hell is well organized, holding board meetings on how to conduct our greatest demise. The good news is, Satan and his army became absolutely powerless at the Cross for *all* who would ever believe in Jesus! Therefore, their influence in our minds is more of an accusatory flavor; a fear-filled sprinkling on top of our current problems, or, on top of our current *peace*. When you *think* and *feel* worthless, guilty, unrighteous, full of angst, and not good enough—or self-righteous and *overly* good enough—more than likely it's coming from the dark realm. But be sure to know it's all smoke and mirrors. Ignore these dingleberries most of the time. Like an annoying barking dog, you can *stomp* at their dumb butts—and they'll scamper off—but don't give them such satisfaction very often. Stay regal, stay classy, because that's what you are, saint (see 2 Timothy 1:7, Revelation 12:10, Mark 5:9,10, 1 John 3:8, 5:18, John 8:44, Hebrews 2:14,15, Luke 10:17, Matthew 4:1-11, James 4:7).

3. **Old, unrenewed thoughts.** When our spirit got saved our gray matter didn't. It will take a lifetime, and then some, of growing in the knowledge of what God has done to our spiritual identity. Amazingly, even though our worrisome mindsets are maturing, our spiritual birth is final! Just the same as our own babies being born from us, we'd never tell them, "You're no longer my child because you keep messing up!" God would never do such a thing either. But even if *we* did, that doesn't mean our child would no longer be our child. Their behavior—holy or not—cannot alter the fact that they have our DNA. Likewise with us and the Father. He knows we are His children and

He's patient with us. Unlike us with our own kids, He will be patient forever because of the New Covenant. Dad keeps no record of our wrongs. He always trusts us and wants the best for us, even when we do dumb stuff. So when our *thinking* doesn't match up with our true nature—which is holy like our Father's—His Spirit continues to counsel us into the truth. Our thoughts *will* mature over time, becoming more confident the more we learn about our true self! These confident thoughts, led by the Spirit, will teach us how to not worry about things we can't control, and instead, just trust Father God! (See John 1:12, 3:6,7,16,17, 10:28, 14:26, 2 Peter 1:4, Matthew 7:11, 1 John 3:1, Ephesians 1:5, Romans 5:1, 8:1,28, 12:2, 1 Corinthians 13:4-8,11, Philippians 1:6, Hebrews 6:16-19, 13:5, 2 Timothy 2:13).

So today, my friends, know this: You can stop worrying so much by thinking about what you're thinking about. Where is that worry coming from? Is it legit? Even if it is, is God still in control? Does He still love you? Are you still His child?...Yes. He's still in control. Yes. He still loves you. *Yes.* You're still His child...Don't worry, friend. Trust God and enjoy your life!

A prayer for you: *Father, today I want to thank you for the renewing of my mind. I know I've only discovered the tip of the iceberg, but I'm SO thankful! Keep teaching me more about who I am because of what Christ has done! Right now, I lift up all who are reading this directly to you. Dad, so many of them are struggling with great worries, you know that. Help them begin to sort through their thoughts and feelings with your grace. Dilute their worries. Your grace will cause them to become focused and*

more courageous! Your grace is sufficient to improve the lives and mindsets of ALL who believe in your Son! Constant worry will be an afterthought when their minds start to match up with your goodness, infinite love, and counseling into WHO they really are—your kids! In Jesus' name I pray, amen.

Day 15

What Happens When You Die?

"For to me, to live is Christ and to die is gain."

Philippians 1:21

Death. I had no plans on writing about this subject. As I type, I'm in the middle of compiling my fifth book, *The Christian Identity, Volume 1*. Over the past eight months I've stored up an index of topics to write about. Each day I thumb through them, choose one, and off I go tapping away on my keyboard. But not today. This subject wasn't in that stack. Instead, the Holy Spirit spoke to me–not in an audible voice, but in an inspiration, in a motivation–and the discussion was this:

"Write about what happens when a person dies."
"How am I supposed to do that? It's a huge mystery. I don't know enough to explain such a thing."
"You know enough."
"What? No. I don't."

"Just write. Trust me."

"Okay."

Paul said to be absent from the body is to be present with the Lord (see 2 Corinthians 5:8). This was the first Bible verse about death that really impacted my knowledge of the afterlife. Even if it was minuscule knowledge, it comforted me. This passage proved there was no such thing as purgatory–as did the words Jesus said to the thief on the cross, "*Today* you will be with me in paradise" (see Luke 23:43).

Today. Not tomorrow, not in a thousand years, not when the living "pray you out of it"–but the *instant* we die, we are in our Creator's presence.

Through my imagination, I could picture myself hitting the eject button on a burning jet plane, and me literally shooting out and up, landing on a cloud where God was hanging out. Neat to think about, but not true. Yes, our spirit comes out of this fragile shell when the body dies, but I believe, based on 2 Corinthians 5:8, we are instantly in the midst of God–uninterrupted–in a completely different realm other than the universe.

God isn't on a cloud. He is Spirit. He is everywhere at all times. He's not bound by time, space, or matter. This is why He's called, "The Alpha and the Omega, the First and the Last, the Beginning and the End" (see Revelation 22:13).

We can't put such an unfathomable God in our "box" of time as we understand it; basing Him on 24-hour rotations of earth, the light and warmth from the sun, and the seasons we live through. *He* created time for us, not the other way around.

Jesus upset the religious, self-centered legalists when He tried to explain the difference in Himself and one of their beloved forefathers:

"Before Abraham was born, I am!" (See John 8:58)

Before Abraham was born, which was way before Jesus was physically born, I *am*? Do you see it, friend? He always has been, and always will be. He temporarily became flesh for *us*. *That* realm He permanently resides in–which has no time frame–is the realm we enter when our flesh can no longer sustain itself. Heaven. What we decide to believe about the Son of God, who came to His very own Creation in the form of His creation, will determine where we spend eternity (see John 1:3, 3:17,18).

The most famous Bible verse of all time explains this truth in detail:

> *"For God so loved the world, that He gave His only begotten Son, that whoever believes in Him shall not perish, but have eternal life."*
> *(John 3:16)*

God *gave* us Jesus–He is the greatest giver *ever*! Why would He give us His only *begotten* Son–as in, from His own supernatural loin? So *we* could have eternal life! Who has eternal life? A life with no beginning or end? Jesus! Therefore, we receive *His* very own life *as* our own! (See Colossians 3:4, Hebrews 7:25).

When we believe Jesus has the ability to forgive us, and that He *has* forgiven us, we literally die in spirit, we get a *new* spirit, and then that spirit is infused with God's Holy Spirit of Christ. We receive His Spirit into our own:

> *"Yet to all who did <u>receive him</u>, to those who <u>believed in his name</u>, he gave the <u>right</u> to become children of God"* (John 1:12)

So–if we've received His Spirit, and His Spirit is in heaven, we are not waiting to "go" to heaven when we die. We're already there. Yes, we eject from this physical realm, but all that's really happening is a *vail* being lifted *so that* we can see clearly…so we can see ourselves as we truly are. Holy. Blameless.

Righteous. Free from all accusations of Satan and people (see Colossians 1:22, 2 Corinthians 5:17,21, Revelation 12:10). Christian, today, right this very moment, because you are infused with Christ, you are *already* in heaven.

"And God <u>raised us up with Christ</u> and seated us <u>with him in the</u> <u>heavenly realms</u> in Christ Jesus" (Ephesians 2:6)

When Paul wrote this to the believers in Ephesus, he was still alive. He hadn't yet died so he was explaining *where* the Ephesians' spirits already *were*: SEATED WITH CHRIST IN HEAVEN!

Spiritually, every human on planet earth is in one of two places. In Adam–whom we descended from after he first sinned, therefore inheriting sinful spirits. Or in Christ, who never sinned. Through one man we became sinful, by no fault of our own; and through another Man we became righteous, by no ability of our own (see Romans 5:12-19).

So if Christ is in heaven and we are in Christ and He is in us–like cereal in milk, and milk in cereal–then we are currently in heaven too. Our physical body isn't but *we* are, our spirit (see Colossians 3:3, 1 Corinthians 6:17,19, 1 John 4:13). We're simply waiting on this particular epoch to be finished so that *we* can no longer be bound by time as well. Since our spirit already *isn't* bound by time–it's in heaven–then all of our sins have been taken away by Christ *from* our spirit. Therefore, when these physical bodies die, we have nothing to fear. We can hug our Creator and look into His eyes with love and gratitude (see 1 John 4:17, Hebrews 9:28).

This universe is temporary, our spirits are *not* temporary and neither is God (obviously). This physical realm has the power of sin and death which entered into it from the moment Adam and Eve no longer believed God (see Romans 5:12, Genesis 4:7). Before that, they were enjoying heaven, uninterrupted. The realm God is in–uninterrupted by sin and death–*is* heaven. John explains this revelation while exiled on the Island of Patmos, teaching us what heaven will be like apart from this fallen planet:

"He will wipe away every tear from their eyes, and death shall be no more, neither shall there be mourning, nor crying, nor pain anymore, for the former things have passed away" (Revelation 21:4)

This might not sound like good news to a behavior-focused person. That is, someone who has worked way too hard "for God" to *not* get rewarded in bunches. Those who got dunked in the most elegant baptismal and repented on the highest levels–but not *too* high, of course. After all, they're not perfect–just *nearly* perfect. Their elitism has a small window for God's finalizing perfection to sneak in and finish things up on their Judgment Day–the day they get paid big bucks!

Oh no, for this group, what I'm teaching here seems too simple and easy. They'll be quick to yell at me, "So Matt, are you saying we can just sin away because we are already in heaven?! How dare you!"

To that, I'd reply, "Where do you see such a thing in my writings? And are *you* saying your *lack* of sinning is causing you to *achieve* heaven? Are you *sure*? Are you absolutely, 100% certain?...Friend, you're not. If you claim to be earning your entrance into heaven by what you do and don't do, then why are you claiming Christ was enough? Why are you *adding* to the Cross? A ticker-tape parade, big mansion, and pot of gold for our wonderful works is not the gospel. I'm sorry. Our reward is Jesus, *now*. Our inheritance is heaven in us, today and forever. This is our only hope of glory. The work has been done. The payment has been made to *each* of us, evenly. It's Him."

The sweet by and by is *here*. The problem is, this person is focused on time as we know it, so they are focused on their behavior in that time frame. Jesus has taken away *all* sins from *every* believer for *all* time–and He *in us* is our full reward! How can this be true? Because He has no beginning or end. Understanding this about Him causes us to sin a whole lot less and enjoy His Spirit a whole lot more because we know we weren't *re*made to sin! Heaven is inside our sinless spirit with Christ so we may as well live Him out! (See Hebrews 7:3, Romans 6:1-14, Galatians 2:20, 5:22,23, Luke 17:21).

Some people are even worried about their physical bodies when they die–as if God still needs them. He doesn't. The truth is, they aren't worth anything once our holy spirits discharge. You can bury them in the ground, or above the ground, send them out to sea like a dead viking–or cremate them. The flesh counts for nothing (see John 6:63). God's grace doesn't end based on what happens to this body when it no longer has a heart beat. It came from dust. It will go back to dust.

"No way, Matt! God needs them for the resurrection! For the new bodies! Cremation is *not* okay!"

Friend, do you honestly believe that God can't make something from nothing? C'mon. Our bodies are going to decay in seven years in a coffin, or seven minutes in a furnace. If someone chooses cremation do you think the Creator can't piece them back together, or form a new body *for* them? The truth is, some people can't even afford a burial. Did Christ say, "It is finished! *Unless* you don't have a nice procession!"?

No. These kind people who are considering cremation simply do *not* want to leave the burden of a large funeral bill to their families. Will our loving Father not give them a new body at the resurrection for being considerate? Of *course* He'll give them a new body–a body just like Jesus' when He was resurrected.

If you go even deeper into this fleshy legalism, some believers are blown up in war, some in acts of terrorism, and others don't even *have* a body–they're obliterated in horrible accidents. Some Christians are washed away in floods, some eaten by wild animals–and in some parts of the world, there's not even a place *for* them to be buried. Geographically it's not possible.

This ideology of cremation not being acceptable to Dad is just plain stupid. Please, recognize where it's coming from: *hell*. Such an ungraceful thought is meant to create fear for children of God, and it's way off base. God's love for us is perfect and perfect love casts out all fear! (See 1 John 4:18, 2 Timothy 1:7).

Paul said, "To live is Christ and to die is gain!" (See Philippians 1:21). What does that mean? It means to *live* on this planet *is* Christ! He was explaining the "vine and branch life" Jesus spoke about in John 15:5! Paul's life was *Christ's* life—as is every believer's when we allow Him to live through us!

… But he also said to die is gain. To *die* is gain. How can that be when we are all striving to live each day? It's because his relationship with God would no longer be interrupted by this universe, by this realm, by this sin-covered planet. The dirty film would be wiped away and he'd finally get see the Father, Son, and Holy Spirit crystal clear. This is why he penned:

> *"No eye has seen, no ear has heard, neither has it even entered into the*
> *mind of man, what God has prepared for those who love Him"*
> *(See 1 Corinthians 2:9)*

We Christians love God—not by what we do or don't do, but by the love He's placed *in* us from the millisecond we first believed. This love in our spiritual makeup is an incorruptible love. It's God Himself. It's heaven (see Ephesians 6:24, Romans 5:5).

We aren't waiting. We are there. Heaven is inside of us.

So today, my friends, know this: What happens when a Christian dies? Our real life begins! What happens when an unbeliever dies? Their real death begins. We either *instantly* begin life uninterrupted with God, or we instantly begin death forever *away* from Him, because of our sin. God can have nothing to do with sin. They don't mix. God and sin is oil and water—peanut butter and pickles. This is why heaven is so amazing—it's because of the complete absence of sin! This is also why we need to be forgiven–it's so Jesus can remove them from us permanently! If you've chosen to believe Christ has forgiven you– then He has, once and for all time–because He's not *bound* by time (see Hebrews 10:10, 2 Peter 3:8). He's taken your sins away, so don't be afraid (see John 1:29, 1 John 3:5). You're already seated with Him in heavenly realms, you're just waiting for this body to finish this short trip to planet earth–a blip on the radar of eternity!…But if you've *not* believed on Jesus, please, do so this very moment. *Today* is your day of salvation! Today! Believe, my friend. Please, please believe. Join us in the relationship for which you were made!

A prayer for you: *Heavenly Father, today I want to thank you for the peace you've given me about my next life. Through your Spirit, I've come to develop a confidence in what Jesus has really done for me. He's given me heaven right now! Yes, to die would be gain, but to live is Him–so let's do this! Right now, I lift up all who are reading this, directly to you. So many of them are believers in Jesus, but are still afraid to die. We are all literally dying every second of the day–some just do it quicker than others. You never meant for us to be here for good, you meant for us to be your ambassadors while briefly visiting. Please ease the minds of these dear readers about death. Help them come to know the truth of what Jesus has finished for them. Expose the amazing abilities of their new, heavenly spirits, which are joined with your Spirit right now! No amount of my most finely-crafted sentences could ever explain heaven, so I didn't even try to do so in this devotional–OUR FINITE MINDS CANNOT FATHOM IT! But we know how to get there! We know how to BE there! The only way is through Christ! In His name I pray, amen.*

Day 16

Christians Can't Backslide

*God has said, "Never will I leave
you; never will I forsake you."*

See Hebrews 13:5

It's impossible for a Christian to backslide. That very word isn't even in the New Testament, which describes the *only* Testament–or *Covenant*–available to planet earth. Don't you think that if backsliding was important it would be mentioned in at least *one* book in the New Testament?

Like tithing, this word has been pulled up and out of the Scriptures written to the Jews–which is now obsolete since Christ brought in the New Covenant at the Cross (see John 19:30, Hebrews 8:6,13). The accusation of "Backslider!" has been forcefully retrofit into the gospel by the supposed Law-abiding citizens, but it doesn't belong and is obviously a turd in the punchbowl.

Jesus' blood set aside the first Covenant *so that* the New Covenant could be established (see Hebrews 10:9). Christians–who were never even a part of the first Covenant–we like to copy/paste the Old onto the New, the phrase *backsliding* included. It's as if we think we're climbing up to God by way of our holy actions and attitudes, then slipping and falling away when we don't have them anymore–or at least on the level others say we should. You know, like *them*.

Most of us are confused with the dividing line of the Covenants–which is the Cross–so we'll pluck out phrases from the Jews' obsolete text and try to shove it into the lives of others as well as our own. Backsliding is no different. But even if we look at the Old Covenant, which was the mail for Israel and nobody else, it's only mentioned twice:

> *"The backslider in heart will be filled with his own ways, But a good man will be satisfied from above." (Proverbs 14:14)*

> *[Healing for the Backslider] And one shall say, "Heap it up! Heap it up! Prepare the way, Take the stumbling block out of the way of My people." (Isaiah 57:14)*

First of all, this was written to the Twelve Tribes–the people group who followed Moses out of slavery in Egypt once Pharaoh set them free. It wasn't written to America, or Canada, or Australia–or the current *country* of Israel, which was founded in 1948–or even you, dear reader. This was written TO THE JEWS UNDER THE OLD COVENANT: ISRAEL. *We* are Gentiles. Everyone who is *not* a Jew *is* a Gentile. If you didn't follow Moses through the Red Sea, this is *not* for you. But even still, for the Jews of old and today, these writings are useless for them too. Now that Christ is here, these documents have become relics! Museum pieces! (See Hebrews 10:26-29).

The only use of Old Testament Scripture is to shut people up–those who *attempt* to obey it and *teach* it. It's meant to push them off the cliff of grace! (See Romans 3:19,20,28, 1 Timothy 1:7-9).

It's fine to look back at Israel's Scripture–to understand the lineage of our Savior and glean from it. But we *must* have our New Covenant glasses on. Anything that causes a Christian fear, is wrong. Christians have *nothing* to fear because fear has to do with punishment and Jesus was punished in full. God is 100% satisfied with His sacrifice (see 1 John 2:2, 4:18, Romans 5:1).

Do unbelievers need to be afraid? Yes. But *not* us.

We are forgiven. We are new creations. We don't have the *ability* to backslide.

After hearing this good news, a kind person might make the statement, "I like what you're saying, Matt. But this is hard to believe. I was saved as a child but then I backslid into sin for 15 years. I turned away and ran from God. My preacher said that hell has the hottest spots reserved for backsliders."

Friend, your preacher is wrong. I'm sure he's a good man and means well. I'd even bet he receives a nice round of applause from his perfectly-behaved people while saying such a thing with big hand movements, a face full of aggression, and a fist-pound on the pulpit.

"Amen, brother! Those nasty backsliders deserve to burn! They know better!"

It preaches good, but biblically, he's not telling the truth.

Once you're saved you can't be unsaved. You don't have that kind of power–a power greater than the Cross, a power greater than a promise between the Father and Son. You might *think* you turned away and ran from God–because of your poor choices and bad attitudes–but you didn't. You did *not* backslide. But even if you *did* slide backwards, because of what the religious people told you, God would slide *with* you. He's in your spirit and will never go away. You've been born again and your identity is final, even if your actions and thoughts don't match up to that finality, which is a process that does not end on this side of the afterlife (see John 3:6,7, Philippians 1:6).

Because of the New Covenant, and your one-time faith in it for your sin, you and your Creator are one. The only thing that could separate you is sin, and Jesus has looked down the timeline of your life and yanked those all away from you (John 1:29, 1 John 3:5, Hebrews 10:10, 2 Peter 3:8). Just look at these amazing promises:

"This is how <u>we know</u> that <u>we live in him and he in us</u>: He has given us of his Spirit." (1 John 4:13)

"But whoever is united with the Lord <u>is one with him</u> in spirit." (1 Corinthians 6:17)

"For you <u>died</u>, and <u>your life is now hidden with Christ in God</u>." (Colossians 3:3)

From the moment you first believed, you *died*. Your sinful spirit, the one you were born with, was supernaturally crucified with Christ, and your new *perfect* spirit is now hidden inside of God *with* Him! Who could possibly find you to harm you if God has hidden you? Nobody! You've been added to the Trinity! (See Galatians 2:20, 2 Corinthians 5:17, Romans 6:6,7, 1 Corinthians 6:11,19, Colossians 2:9,10, 1 John 5:8, John 14:20, 17:21).

Therefore, you don't have the supernatural ability to live *in* sin because God can have nothing to do with sin–and you're inside of Him and He's in you! (See 1 John 3:9). Sure, you can walk according to the flesh–which can be influenced by the *power* of sin–the force. You can even take your physical shell to places in which sinful activity is happening in bunches–but God goes *with* you, never to leave you nor forsake you! (See Hebrews 13:5). Because of your one-time belief in the event at Calvary, your spirit is sealed up and secure! No sin can ever enter into it again! Just look!

"And you also were included in Christ when you heard the message of truth, the gospel of your salvation. When you believed, you were marked in him with a seal, the promised Holy Spirit" (Ephesians 1:13)

You've been marked with a seal! God's very own Spirit-stamp! Nobody has the strength to break this royal seal, not even you! When demonic forces and self-centered people want you to believe that your sinning is breaking God's seal–or making it weak–the grace found *in* that seal causes it to grow larger! (See Romans 5:20, Ephesians 2:8,9). The only way this seal could ever be broken is if Jesus dies again, and we are nuts if we're on board with such a theology! (See Hebrews 7:25-27).

The Father's promise to the Son, and the Son's promise to the Father *at* the Cross, has caused you to inherit a new spirit and become a member of heaven for good! *This* is what we gotta deal with–not dealing with sin–but dealing with permanent righteousness! (See Hebrews 1:3, 6:16-19, 2 Corinthians 5:21, Colossians 1:22, Ephesians 1:5, John 1:12, 3:18).

"But Matt, I *feel* like I still backslide when I sin."

…I hear you. I really do. When I sin, I too can easily allow myself to feel like I've slid away from God. But those are just feelings. Feelings can't override the Cross. It's good to have remorse for sin, we weren't made for it. But no amount of remorse can keep us saved, cause us to be more forgiven, *or* more sanctified than we are right now. It's healthy and *natural* as a sinless spirit, a saint, to feel bad when we temporarily go insane and act according to stuff that is not of faith. But feelings didn't save us, and they don't keep us saved. Jesus' life does (see Colossians 3:4, John 3:16,17, Hebrews 10:14).

Feelings are like a breeze, they come and go without invitation or eviction. They're just…*feelings*…a part of our soul. They don't determine truth or error. The Spirit within us does. Sometimes we can feel like we're backsliding far from God because of the lies we've been taught about our unholy behaviors and thoughts–there's quite a bit to unlearn. But as we learn, we are *still* holy. We're not changing–we've *been* changed! Instead, we are maturing into our real self's abilities and attributes (see 1 Corinthians 13:11, Philippians 1:6, Romans 12:2).

The truth is, if we were actually backsliding then that would mean we would be climbing *up* to God, each and every day. We'd be striving to crest an impossible-to-summit, huge, infinite mountain. We are not climbing…We are resting in the green pastures at the bottom of that mountain, with Jesus. *He* climbed down to *us*, so that *we* would never have to climb up to Him–because He knows we couldn't. That's how much He cares. Christ did everything we never could, out of love.

So today, my friends, know this: God has made His home inside of every believer! If we think we're sliding away from Him, we're not! We might be sliding away from overbearing people and ungraceful double-talk. We might be sliding away from the "Be like me!" teachings–but not from God! We may have even slid away from *knowing* who we are as children of God– but not from God! The word backslide is one of the most behavior-centered, non-Christ-focused words on the demonic market. If it's in your vocabulary repertoire, dump it. You don't need it. No amount of incorrect actions and attitudes could ever cause a Christian to slide away from the promises made at the Cross!

A prayer for you: *Dad, I know you remember the days of me begging you to come back to me as I lived by my feelings–but you never left to begin with. Satan had me so deceived about your grace. The truth is, even when I feel like I'm faithless, you remain faithful because you cannot disown Christ in*

me, OR me. Your Word says so in 2 Timothy 2:13, and I believe it. Thank you for such a rock-solid confidence in what you've done for me! Right now, I lift up all who are reading this, directly to you. Father, so many of them have been innocently duped into Old Covenant/New Covenant-copy/ paste theology–as if they're doing something, or NOT doing something, to keep you near. Nothing could be further from the truth! It is by their BIRTH you stay near! It is by their BIRTH they continue in your love! It is by their birth you will never let them slide away! Where we go, you go! Teach us and counsel us into even deeper revelations of this amazing, graceful relationship, that we have with you through Christ! Amen.

Day 17

Demonic Possession, Private Prayer Language, and Die to Self

*"See to it that no one takes you captive through
hollow and deceptive philosophy, which depends
on human tradition and the elemental spiritual
forces of this world rather than on Christ."*

Colossians 2:8

As the years go by and I learn more about God's grace it's easier to listen to teachings which do not match *up* to His grace. This doesn't mean that as I listen I have my belief *about* His grace swayed, it just means I can listen to error without being angry at the person teaching it. It means I can see the person teaching the opposite *of* God's grace *with* God's grace–which is what I'm supposed to do–and honestly, what feels most natural to me as a child of God.

Such a renewal of this part of my thinking has taken a very long time. For years, the Holy Spirit was trying to teach me to calm down when I'd hear a sermon that was off base, rather than resent the person teaching it, and rather than head for the hills. I was angry over the lies *about* God's grace, when I should have been anchored *in* His grace. That is, in my thinking. Now I can easily sit through something I don't agree with and still think of that teacher with love and respect. How? Because I know we will *all* be learning and growing in our Creator's grace, not just in this lifetime, but on into eternity. With this renewed mindset I can "eat the meat and spit out the bones" when listening to anyone.

Recently, I sat through a sermon in which red flag after red flag was popping up in my spirit. The gist of the grinding words were three main subjects: demonic possession, private prayer language, and die to self.

I'm sure this person meant well, but I'd like to express what God has revealed to me through the truths of the New Covenant:

1. **They made the claim that a Christian had a demonic manifestation right in front of them.** For most of my life I would have eaten this up with a spoon and asked for seconds. But God has taught me that a *Christian* cannot be possessed by a demon. Why? Because we are literally possessed by *Christ's* Spirit, our spirits are sealed up and protected *by* His Spirit, and our spirits are 100% His possession (see 1 Corinthians 6:17,19 Ephesians 1:13, 1 Peter 2:9). The apostle John said the enemy cannot even touch us (see 1 John 5:18). The only thing he or his demons can do is *accuse* us in our minds and *tempt* us (see Revelation 12:10, Matthew 4:3). But still, he is a liar and doesn't have the ability to accuse us or tempt us with any truth (see John 8:44). So it's best to just ignore him most of the time. The Cross has completely disarmed the forces of hell for all who believe in Christ's forgiveness! (See 1 John 3:8, John 3:16). Satan and his crew are now but toothless, old, barking dogs, behind a fence, who are about to be

euthanized, never to pester a child of God again. All they can do is lie to you about who you *really are* in Christ, because they *see* who you really are in the spiritual realm as a heaven-ready person. Therefore, they will lie to you *about* you, or they'll try to tickle your ears by making you believe *what* you are doing–or not doing–is earning, improving, or sustaining your righteousness. Just like with Adam and Eve, Satan wants you to think you have the knowledge of good and evil so that you can be "more" like God, when you already *are* like God in full because of your faith in Jesus Christ! (See 1 John 4:17). The demons are well aware that your righteousness is just as free *now* as it was from the moment you first believed–even if *you* are not aware of this! (See Romans 5:1, 6:6,7, 8:1, 2 Corinthians 5:17,21, Hebrews 10:10, 1 Corinthians 6:11). So either this person who was acting like they were demonically possessed was not a Christian, or they were a Christian who was exuding an incorrect learned behavior. The truth is, God won't share you with any demon. There's not a single verse in the New Testament where a Christian is having a demon cast out of them. In fact, just the opposite, they are afraid of us! (See Luke 10:17, Mark 3:13-15, James 2:19, 1 John 4:4).

2. **They claimed they had to speak in a private prayer language to cast the demon out.** Again, there is no record of this in the New Testament. Further, if this person is referencing tongues, don't you think that if the need to speak in a foreign language *we do not know* (which is what tongues is, see Acts 2:8) was necessary to cast out a demon who doesn't *need* to hear a foreign language, this would have been written in at least *one* of the epistles? James, John, Peter, Paul, none of them instruct the churches to do this. In fact, there is no passage in *any* of their letters which records the need for a private prayer language. God understands *all* languages, so there's no reason to speak in a foreign

language when we pray. Sure, the Holy Spirit prays for us in groans we cannot fathom in our human minds, but when Paul said this *in context,* he was saying the Holy Spirit prays for us *when we don't know what to pray for* (see Romans 8:26). Have you ever had times when life is so difficult you don't know what to pray? I have. And when we are in these stages of severe angst and turmoil, the Holy Spirit personally advocates for us *to* the Father. Friend, there's no need to speak in tongues to rid a demon from our midst. All we need to say is the name of Jesus! We'd be remiss to think our human effort, forced or faked repeated babble, foreign languages, or even our many words can sway the demons of hell. Only Christ can do this through us! We have no need *whatsoever* to be afraid of any demon! Jesus lives in us and we have His very power! (See Luke 10:19).

3.   **They claimed what we need to do as Christians is "die to self."** This phrase is worn out by the body of Christ and is not correct. There's not a single verse in any epistle advising believers to die to self. It's just not there. On the contrary, we are informed *repeatedly* to live! (See Colossians 3:4, Ephesians 5:15,16, 2 Corinthians 5:7, John 6:35, 7:38, Hebrews 12:14, James 3:13, Galatians 2:20, 5:25, 1 John 4:9,15, 1 Timothy 4:12, 1 Corinthians 15:22, Philippians 1:21, and more!). We are informed over and over that we need to learn *who* we are–what the New Covenant has done to us–and then *be* that person! (See Romans 12:2, Philippians 1:6, 2:12, 4:8, Hebrews 8:13, 10:10, 2 Corinthians 3:18, 1 Peter 1:16, Galatians 5:22,23). Christ said He came so we can have life–not daily death! (See John 10:10). Yes, we are putting to death old *mindsets* daily, but we do this by living *out* our true selves! (See 2 Peter 1:4). We–our identity–we are holy, blameless saints! (See Colossians 1:22, Hebrews 10:14). It is when we learn more *about* our free sainthood–which is righteousness given to us by

supernatural rebirth (see John 3:5-7)–we will *then* live organically much more often than not! We will live out who we believe we are! This is why "die to self" is absent from Scripture. In 1 Corinthians 15:31, Paul said he "faces death every day." But he was talking about the dangers he encountered while spreading the gospel, not about his incorrect actions and attitudes. Go read around that verse and you'll see. And in Romans 6:6, he said our old self died–it was crucified–and we got a *new* self! A self who is joined with Christ's own Spirit! This is why we are advised to present ourselves as *living* sacrifices, not daily dead ones! (See Romans 12:1). Therefore, live! You are fully equipped to live the life that God has put inside of you–Jesus! (See 2 Peter 1:3, Galatians 2:20).

So today, my friends, know this: Christian, you are complete, holy, and sealed up with God's Spirit forever! No demon can touch you! You are actually hidden *inside* of Christ! (See Colossians 2:10, 3:3). You don't need a special person saying foreign languages over you to cast *out* a demon either–you *are* that special person whom no demon can mess with! Be confident in this truth! More importantly, you don't need to keep dying to self each day. You have a good self, a righteous self, a blameless self. You simply need to learn more about who you truly are, and then live your life to the fullest!

A prayer for you: *Heavenly Father, thank you for teaching me the truth of your grace. I want to learn more and more about it! Through such grace-filled knowledge, I have been set free from so many incorrect doctrines. Thank you. Right now, I lift up all who are reading this, directly to you.*

Please begin to open up their minds to the graceful easiness that lies within them if they believe–which is your Spirit. And for the person whom I referenced in this devotional, take them deeper into what Christ has really done for them. They used the verse in John 12:24–of a kernel having to go into the ground and die so it can produce many more seeds–as an example of us having to die daily. But this is out of context according to your Word. Jesus was talking about Himself, not us. The previous verse explains this, as does your promise to Abraham in Genesis 17:4-7, and Paul even talked about your seed being Christ in Galatians 3:29. It was JESUS who needed to die so that WE could receive His Spirit into EACH of us! WE are those new seeds! Through your New Covenant with mankind, we only die ONCE in spirit, and we receive our new life in Christ at the very same time! Thank you for this free gift of life–Christ's life! Empower us to live Him out! In Jesus' name, amen.

Day 18

Why We Shouldn't Be Grace Jerks

"They will know you by your love." ~Jesus

See John 13:35

Getting friend requests from random people is the norm on social media now. So when this happens I'll open up the request, see if the profile isn't ISIS posing as a 19-year-old "lonely" female, and then take a peak at their time-line and mutual friends. If they aren't being tagged in Ray-Ban Sunglass memes repeatedly, or sharing lots of political posts, I'll normally accept the request.

Because of Facebook's frustrating algorithms, the odds of me even seeing a friend's post regularly, is rare. Oh how I miss being able to see every person's—and *Page's* post—in order, *when* they post! Back then—in "the good old days" of Facebook—you didn't have to worry about not seeing what *you* want to see. Now Facebook determines who and what shows up in your feed. To make matters even worse, if you want to see a Page's post when they post, or ever, you have to make it a See First. Even then, you can only have so many of those See Firsts … but I digress.

One day I opened up a request from a man, scanned the profile, and accepted. It wasn't two minutes later I received a message from him insulting a certain group of Christians. From what he was advertising on his timeline, I thought he was a grace guy.

"Oh well," I said to myself. I took it as no big deal, didn't reply or agree with him, and got on with my day.

Over the months that followed, I witnessed from this person very condescending, aggressive posts, which "claimed" the backing of God's grace. I never got involved in any of them, but one day I made a comment and the guy immediately ripped into me. I didn't respond but twice, and I could feel myself starting to get angry. Anger over grace is a red flag for me to be silent and back off. It doesn't happen often, but when it does, I can tell nothing good will come from continuing on.

The Holy Spirit was nudging me to just let it go, while the enemy was doing the opposite. I chose self-control and moved along. I'm guessing this man wanted to keep letting me know how amazing his knowledge was about God's grace because he messaged me privately once I unfollowed the post. I didn't respond to that message either.

Crossing my boundaries once more, he messaged me *again.* I blocked him.

Still feeling the need to make sure I believed exactly like he did, he messaged me on my Facebook ministry Page. I overlooked that paragraph too. I marked it as "read" and didn't even scan it. Yet again he messaged me in a private email on my ministry website. Like his other correspondences, I didn't allow myself to look at what he typed up. The first sentence of each message was enough to know his distain for my thoughts about God's grace–and about *me.*

Why was this man so rude about letting me know how *right* he was about God's grace, yet he refused to give that very same grace *away* to me? I don't know. That's something he will have to figure out with God. But I do know this: *I wasn't about to take the bait and retaliate.*

For too many years of my life I would have spent hours being *ungraceful about* God's grace *to* this person who didn't *understand* God's grace. Do you see my hypocrisy? I lived out my faith refusing to give away the grace in which I was so passionate about receiving. Then I went from one extreme to the other. I started to act like a grace hippie and completely ignored unacceptable behavior. My past struggles with codependency issues inflamed this out-of-balance time in my life. My mind was being renewed and I didn't understand yet that God wants us to be *gracefully* well-balanced. When we're not, the enemy can get his way with our actions and attitudes (see 1 Peter 5:8).

Jesus said people will know us by our love, not by our "awesome" biblical knowledge or our *interpretation* of biblical knowledge (see John 5:39, 13:35). Even if we *think* our knowledge is graceful, love is the true barometer. I've witnessed some Christians enamored with the grace of God–they get it. Yet they absolutely refuse to give that same grace away to those who disagree with them about the White House.

I did this. Just looking back on my Facebook memories from the last election and reading some of my posts I cringe. *"What was my problem? Why did I have to say that so rudely?"* I had forgotten who I was. I could have easily said things in a more graceful way and got the same points across. But condescending remarks is exactly what happens when we attempt to express ourselves without grace.

Even when we are setting healthy boundaries, grace *can* be the foundation. When it's not, we have forgotten our true selves. Peter explains this truth to the early Christians:

> *"For this very reason, make every effort to add to your faith goodness; and to goodness, knowledge; and to knowledge, self-control; and to self-control, perseverance; and to perseverance, godliness; and to godliness, mutual affection; and to mutual affection, love. For <u>if you possess these qualities in increasing measure</u>, they will keep you from being ineffective*

and unproductive in your <u>knowledge</u> of our Lord Jesus Christ. But whoever <u>does not have them</u> is nearsighted and blind, <u>forgetting that they have been cleansed</u> from their past sins." (2 Peter 1:5-9)

So today, my friends, know this: Don't forget that you *have been* cleansed. Remembering this will allow your knowledge of Christ to *increase*. The truth is, no Christian is a grace jerk. When we act like grace jerks that's exactly what we're doing–*acting*. No part of our true self is rude! No part of our true self is condemning or impatient! No part of our true self has to angrily *defend* ourselves! We love people–from the heart! We don't have to straighten everyone out! Our job is to simply express Christ at all times, and this happens naturally as we just *be* ourselves. So Christian, be *you*.

A prayer for you: *Father, thank you for teaching me more about who I am. I am full of your grace! It's been an amazing journey to understanding there's no pressure on me to iron-out the world's view of you. You've got that handled just fine! Your Spirit is the only true and authentic Teacher! Right now, I lift up all who are reading this, directly to you. Dad, please reveal to these dear readers that they will expose you in the greatest ways possible, by loving people. Grace flows FROM your love, and when we feel the most like ourselves, it's when we are loving people. Open up the minds of those who have forgotten who they are! HEAL the minds of those who have been hurt by others who were incorrectly expressing your love! Bring us all together so we can change the world WITH your love and grace! In Christ's name, amen.*

Day 19

How Legalism Destroys Families

*"Christ is the end of the Law, in order to bring
righteousness to everyone who believes."*

Romans 10:4

Part of the recovery process for my past battle with alcoholism is to watch the A&E TV series, *Intervention*. It reminds me of just how bad my addiction was and the despair I was in as a functioning, successful person, who struggled with drinking too much.

If you've never watched it, the premise is this: a documentary crew follows around someone fighting an addiction. Unbeknownst to them, at the end, an intervention occurs.

I studied this show for years, trying to figure out how these extremely addicted people finally got sober. I *longed* for sobriety, envying their "sobriety date" each time I saw it before the credits ran. Sadness always overtook my emotions when they relapsed or went back to their addiction. Sometimes the recap text at the end–rather than the day they got sober and how they were doing–would be *when* they had died. Those episodes would take me even deeper into desperately wanting freedom from my own prison cell of alcoholic tendencies.

Then I finally got it! *My* sobriety date! May 8th, 2014! Praise God!

I was recently laying on my couch taking in an episode about an addicted man whose family was extremely legalistic. He wanted nothing to do with that, and acted out, fighting back against their extreme condemnation with rebellion. Regularly shaming him to no end–because he wasn't "good like his brother"–this kind man turned to booze to numb the pain of being a severe disappointment to his parents.

Part of his issue was he had caught his devout "perfectly behaved" father having an affair in the act. His world instantly crumbled as he witnessed, in his own words, his "idol having sex with a coworker." To make matters worse, he confronted his dad about it, told his mom, and his father grounded him for three months while calling him a liar. Can you believe that? I can. Self-righteously-minded people do everything they possibly can to hide nasty behavior because *holy* behavior is where they find their identity.

As children of God our identity is in our birth not in our behavior. That sentence will stir up legalistic demons who hang out with grace-confused people. When we flip-flop the two–birth and behavior–or attempt to mix them, we hurt those around us including ourselves. Our birth-focus must come *first* then behavior *from* that birth, second. This is the sweet spot of the Christian life where peace and confidence resides.

As I watched this young man being interviewed by the producers with tears streaming down his face, it was easy to see he wasn't lying about his dad's affair. Why would he make up such a thing? He had nothing to gain and everything to lose. The pain in his voice while telling the tale, and how he was treated by his overbearing, religious family, was heart-wrenching. He was taught to always tell the truth, he *does* tell the truth, and gets punished by the man who taught him *to* tell the truth…Why? Legalism. The self-made law of "What will people think?"

His dad refused to admit what he had done. "This would damage my reputation at church, so I'm not talking about it," he said during a close-up. At one point, he glared at the interviewer, took off his mic, and walked out of the room. But that's what legalism does. It says, "Look at me! I'm doing everything right! *I'm* your perfect example!" And *when* we fail our bogus identity fails too–which is devastating. In turn, we abuse people and frantically scramble while trying to keep our fake prestige intact. False humility or hypocrisy follows suit *rather* than refocusing on our true sinless identity.

Legalism was destroying this family and the enemy was sitting back with a grin *watching* while eating a big bowl of popcorn. "Ha! This is great! They think that what they're doing is making them right with God! And the boy is constantly getting drunk because of it! YESSSSSS!"

One of Satan's greatest deceptions is to make us *think* we're defined by our actions and religious knowledge. Nothing could be further from the truth as even the devil has the Bible memorized (see Matthew 4:5-7). Only our supernatural birth defines us. This birth happens *once* by grace through faith in Jesus' ability to forgive us. When we believe He *has* forgiven us, this act of faith causes our spirit to die and instantly be reborn as perfect–as righteous–*just* as perfectly righteous as Christ Himself! (See John 1:12, 3:6,7, Ephesians 2:8,9, 1 John 4:17, Hebrews 10:10,14).

Free righteousness is what the gospel is! *Understanding* our free righteousness allows us to grow in maturity because we know our holy identity can never be altered or reversed! (See Romans 3:21,22, 2 Corinthians 5:17, 2 Timothy 2:13). So when we mess up it's not that big of a deal due to the fact that we *know* who we really are. We are *not* our mess-ups, we are *not* our successes, we are saints! Wallowing in guilt doesn't honor God, nor does covering stuff up! Getting up, dusting off, and moving forward *as* our true self, does!

Satan wants us to not only think we are defined by our good actions, but even more, by our bad actions. Just as long as we aren't seeing ourselves as we truly are: *coheirs with Christ* (see Romans 8:17). However, if we can allow a great divorce to happen in our minds–separating our *who* from our *do*–we can begin enjoying life to the fullest and so can our loved ones!

The dad in this episode of Intervention mistakenly had his identity confused with his actions. His son was drowning himself in alcohol because of the pain this was causing. The most liberating thing his father could have done, for everyone involved, was admit to the affair, admit that choice was *not* who he really was, and then moved on.

Such an act of humility would've brought more healing for his family than he realizes. He would've felt better than he'll ever know. We never feel more like ourselves than when we are exuding God's Spirit. His Spirit is meek and humble, expressing Him is where we find the deepest levels of rest (see Matthew 11:29, John 15:5).

So today, my friends, know this: In order to love your family in the most authentic way possible, be yourself. As a Christian, you have everything you need on the inside to love others how God wants you to, and truthfully, how *you* want to as well. You want what God wants. We don't need to hide our mistakes or belittle them. When we mess up, the best thing we can do is admit it, learn, and grow. Never allow the enemy to convince you that your actions define you! Birth defines you! Birth into God's family! Genuine actions only come by way of growing in this truth!

A prayer for you: *Father, today I want to thank you for the freedom found in understanding who I am. I know I'll still be learning even after I leave this body, but I'm so grateful for the truth! You know I struggled for so long with not only an addiction to alcohol, but also to legalism. What*

misery the enemy had me in! Thank you for teaching me my identity and how to live a balanced life! Right now, I lift up all who are reading this, directly to you. So many of them are confused. They've been taught that what they do and don't do, defines them. The truth is, YOU define them. As a believer in Christ, you say they are holy, righteous, blameless, and set apart. Help them begin to understand these truths so authentic behaviors and attitudes can follow. In Christ's name I pray, amen.

Day 20

You Will Know Them by Their Fruits?

*"Beware of false prophets, who come to you in
sheep's clothing but inwardly are ravenous wolves.
You will recognize them by their fruits."*

See Matthew 7:15,16

Certain people like to call *other* people "false prophets" if their theology doesn't match up perfectly with their own. On social media, in their frustration, they'll blurt this out with multiple exclamation points as they get into a thumb war. Isn't it amazing how angry the enemy can get a person when they don't understand God's grace? His grace puts *out* fires, legalism stokes them.

The opening passage of this devotional, found in the middle of Matthew 7, is a staple food set of verses for those who struggle with behavioralism. Even I was taught growing up that we should be inspecting people's "fruits." However, Jesus isn't referencing Christians in this passage. Instead, He's talking about those who refused to place their faith in Him–the teachers of the Law who were considered, to Jesus, false prophets. Why were they called false prophets? Because the true Prophets prophesied about *Him* (see Matthew 7:15, John 1:45).

Therefore, as Christians, we aren't known by our fruits, but by our *fruit*– the fruit of the Spirit of Christ inside of us:

> *"But the fruit of the Spirit is love, joy, peace, patience, kindness, goodness, faithfulness, gentleness and self-control. Against such things there is no law." (Galatians 5:22,23)*

Unlike the Pharisees' outward signs, or fruits, *these* qualities Paul wrote about cannot be measured or legislated because they're not coming from our effort but Christ's within. This is what makes *the fruit of the Spirit* different than *fruits* which grow from obeying the Mosaic Law–which included the Ten Commandments and tithing (see 2 Corinthians 3:3,6,7, Romans 7:8, Matthew 23:23).

If you'll peek back up at those two verses from Galatians, notice what I've underlined. *Against such things there is no law.* Why would Paul throw this in after listing off all of the amazing expressions of Christ within us? Because the people in Galatia were being taught, incorrectly, to sprinkle in some Law with their Jesus. Paul wanted to be sure they understood that the Law had no part in their lives, not even a dollop (see Galatians 5:9).

But for those who were still doing this, he calls them fools and then reminds them of how they first received the Holy Spirit:

> *"You foolish Galatians! Who has bewitched you? Before your very eyes Jesus Christ was clearly portrayed as crucified. I would like to learn just one thing from you: Did you receive the Spirit by the works of the Law, or by believing what you heard?" (Galatians 3:1,2)*

So if Paul is calling the Galatians fools for dipping their toe into the Law, and Jesus exposed Law teachers as false prophets–ravenous wolves in sheep's clothing (see Matthew 7:15)–then why should we be focused on outward appearances and actions? The answer is, we shouldn't. Even God isn't focused on fruits, but instead, our hearts:

> *"The LORD does not look at the things people look at. People look at the outward appearance, but the LORD looks at the heart."*
> *(See 1 Samuel 16:7)*

Christians have *good* hearts, and this is where our fruit comes from!

"You're lying, Matt! The heart is deceitfully wicked!"

Friend, yes it is, *without* faith in Christ. Once we've placed our belief in Jesus as our Savior, we receive new hearts which are exactly like His. They're no longer wicked, but infused with the Spirit of God (see Ezekiel 36:26, Hebrews 8:10, 10:16, Colossians 3:3, 1 Corinthians 6:17).

"So are you saying we can just sin all we want?! That right and wrong doesn't matter?! And that we *shouldn't* be known by our good morals?! How dare you!"

That's not what I'm saying at all. Do you see where your focus is? Do you see what you're finding *your* identity in? Fruit inspection and fruit comparison. It's upsetting when this is threatened *if* we are keeping track of fruit score.

With all due respect, the truth is we don't even *want* to sin. This is why we struggle when we do. Unbelievers have no problem with sinning, they have naturally wicked hearts (see 1 John 3:9). *We've* become obedient to God *from* the heart (Romans 6:17). We can't get away from our heavenly want-to because of the New Covenant. We've been spiritually reprogrammed–even more, *recreated*–to *not* sin. So all of the sinful stuff we try to force? *That* isn't coming from Christ inside of us who *is* our obedience. Instead, it's coming from the power of sin which is everywhere on planet earth like a vaporous wet blanket (Romans 1:5, 5:12, 16:26).

When we attempt to force sinful actions and attitudes *from* us, it's the same as trying to force a penguin to enjoy the beach–it's just not natural. It never will be, so just don't do it. But–doing so won't cause us to become sinful, just the same as placing that penguin on a beach won't cause it to become a seagull.

As for morals? Our morals are a joke. Why? Because if we want to live by morals as our guide we must be perfect like God is perfect–good luck with that (see Matthew 5:48). Morals is exactly what the Pharisees, who followed the Law, were focused on. Jesus never said, "They will know you by your morals." He said, "They will know you by your *love*" (see John 13:35).

Legalistic demons want you fixated on morals so you can *judge* others by them. The Spirit wants you focused on love, so you can *love* others by *Him*. Jesus touched on this subject with the fruit-inspecting Law-lovers:

> *"Do not judge, or you too will be judged. For in the same way you judge others, you will be judged, and with the measure you use, it will be measured to you. Why do you look at the speck of sawdust in your brother's eye and pay no attention to the plank in your own eye? How can you say to your brother, 'Let me take the speck out of your eye,' when all the time there is a plank in your own eye? You hypocrite, first take the plank out of your own eye, and then you will see clearly to remove the speck from your brother's eye." (Matthew 7:1-5)*

An even deeper look into the false prophets mentioned in Matthew 7– who were against Christ as the Messiah–*they* were called trees, yet *we* are called branches (see Matthew 7:17-20, John 15:5). Trees do everything on their own, they are completely self-sufficient. Branches can do nothing on their own, they have no life without the vine. Do you see the difference on dependence? We are trusting Christ to produce *His* fruit! They are trusting themselves to produce *their* fruits! This is huge!

God doesn't know a *Christian* by the good things we do–or *produce*! Lots of unbelievers do amazing things! They produce good stuff! Philanthropic fruits galore! *Religious* fruits galore! But those are fruits, not *fruit* of the Spirit! Do you see it?! There's a difference! They want to be known by what they do! For saints, our Father knows us by birth! God recognizes us by our supernatural lineage! By our heaven-ready identity! (See John 1:12, 3:6,7,16, Romans 8:1,17, 1 John 3:1, Ephesians 1:5, Matthew 7:21-23).

It is from this natural state of *being*–as God's very own spiritual offspring–we *do* the most wonderful things! We enjoy life to the fullest! Powerful stuff comes *out* from *within* us! Forgiving, enthusiastic, *graceful* things we've never said or done before, now happen all the time! An unparalleled *strength* we didn't know was there, is there! Amazing feats fall left and right from our wake! Loving, patient, kind actions and attitudes in which we didn't even know we had the ability to pull *off*, now flow *out* every single day! Not because we are *known* by this fruit, but because this fruit is coming from *being* known by a God with an unconditional love for us! The very God of the universe who is our doting Dad!

So today, my friends, know this: We are not called to be fruit inspectors or producers. We are called to be branches. Do branches look down the vine, constantly measuring each other up? Nope. We all simply *enjoy* the vine while loving Him and loving the other branches who are connected. From this love, we show those who are *not* connected, how amazing the branch life truly is.

A prayer for you: *Heavenly Father, thank you for teaching me that I'm not responsible to inspect or produce fruits, as if I work for Dole or Del Monte. What an easy way to live! You don't inspect fruits either, you look at our hearts! What a good Dad you are! Right now, I lift up all who are reading this, directly to you. For those who are incorrectly obsessed with the behavior of others, as well as themselves, give them relief today. Let them know you'll take care of that stuff and all they need to do is find rest in Christ. If they believe in Him, they already have that rest and are in no need of finding it! They just need to begin enjoying it! Teach them how, Father! Teach them how to relax in who Jesus is, and in who they are in Him! We love you. Amen.*

Day 21

How Can I Know Good from Evil?

"For God knows that when you eat from it your eyes will be opened, and you will be like God, knowing good and evil." ~Satan

Genesis 3:5

Adam and Eve wanted to be self-righteous, literally. Their desire was to have the ability to point out the difference in good and evil, sin and not sin. Their disobedience was "no longer believing God about who they already were"–just like some of today's Christians. But for us, who we already *are*.

Although the force of sin didn't enter our realm until they first chose this (see Romans 5:12), determining what sin is–*exactly*–was Satan's original temptation. He said they "will be" like God, but only if they knew good and evil according to him, according to the devil. He lied *about* God then lied about *them*. Just look at these distortions of truth:

"For God knows that when you eat from it your eyes will be opened, and you <u>will be</u> like God, knowing good <u>and</u> evil." (Genesis 3:5)

The fact was, they were *already* like God. They were perfect. To this day, the enemy lies to Christians about their spiritual perfection just the same as he lied to Adam and Eve *before* they were sinful. He wants us to think we need to do more to stay perfect, or that knowledge will make us "more" perfect. After biting on that bait, he flips the script and convinces us no matter *what* we do we'll never *be* perfect. Wrong.

Here's the truth about you, Christian: your spirit is perfectly cleansed forever by grace through faith in one Sacrifice–Jesus' (see Ephesians 2:8,9, Hebrews 10:10,14).

The first humans were created impeccable because that's how God creates things. This couple didn't need to become lord of their own ring by looking to *themselves*–led by Satan–to determine good and evil. But the devil falsely advertised, and they pulled out their checkbook to purchase.

Their spirit–which was born from God completely sinless–as well as God's Spirit *with* them *guiding* them, was all they needed for life and godliness. Knowing right from wrong according to the serpent was fool's gold. Same with us Christians. We don't need his religious advice, or non-religious. We only require counseling from the Holy Spirit within (see 2 Corinthians 3:8, John 14:26).

Even the words in the Bible can be influenced by Satan if the Spirit isn't escorting us as we read (see John 5:39,40, Luke 4:9-11).

Adam and Eve no longer believed God, they wanted to be able to determine the difference in good and evil *apart* from God. This is why He asked them a rhetorical question, "Who *told* you that you were naked?" (See Genesis 3:11, my emphasis added). God already knew it was Satan and He wanted to point this out. They *weren't* naked and didn't need any fig leaves. They were flawless in every way! But the enemy put the lie in their heads, "Something is bad wrong with you. Hurry, cover up or hide from God."

Sadly, they believed him. Sadly, this continues today for many children of God. We are so focused on judging others according to our own definition of good and evil. We say things like:

"Just be like me. Never miss church. Sit close to the front. Never question pastor. If someone has been to seminary they know much more than you, so obey them or else. Volunteer all the time because this stores up your treasures in heaven. You want to get paid BIG TIME on Judgment Day, don't you? Give until it hurts. Get up early to read your Bible and follow my lead because I'm a godly person. My sins aren't as bad as others; I'll tell you if yours are. Just do what I do and you'll be on the right track to pleasing God. My level is what you need to get on. I know the difference in good and evil. After all, I've been doing this a while now, so pay attention. If you need something, let me know and I'll pray for you. God hears me because of my dedication and obedience."

Friend, those are fig leaves. Each sentence above is just the same as Adam and Eve's covering, none of which would've made them acceptable to God. They were infected with sin. Unfortunately, God can have nothing to do with sin and no amount of camouflage could take their sin away nor manage it. The Fall had happened.

"So Matt, why didn't God just deal with Adam and Eve's sin Himself. I mean, He's God. He can do anything. Why not take it away as soon as it happened?"

This is a great question, one I battled with myself for quite some time. His Spirit has taught me that God *couldn't* step in and remove their sin because He had given dominion of this physical realm to man (see Genesis 1:26-28).

Man brought sin in, so man would have to deal with sin. God can't lie, so He was unable to go back on His word of giving all authority of this planet to us. Therefore, to solve this problem *for* us, He *became* man to set us free from the sin *we* caused. That's how much He loves us. He belittled Himself by becoming lower than even the angels. Born as a human, He played by His own rules so that we could have eternal life! (See Hebrews 2:9, Colossians 1:15).

Banishing sin once and for all time–for every human who would believe–Christ took on sin *in* His own human body; a body which did not deserve death because it never sinned. He *became* sin as a man so that we could become sinless as God's children (see Genesis 3:15, John 3:16, 2 Corinthians 5:19,21, Galatians 4:4, Romans 5:6-12, 6:23).

In essence, when God said, "Who told you that you were naked?" He was saying, "Who told you something was wrong with you to begin with? I created you just like me."

His Spirit bears this same witness to every born-again believer on planet earth: "Nothing is wrong with you, child."

To make matters worse, Adam and Eve thought their actions of hiding and blaming would cover their nakedness, which was another fabrication from hell. No amount of actions, religious or not, can cover our sinfulness *before* we believe in Christ. So *after* we believe, no amount can *un*cover us. We've been supernaturally reborn just the same as Adam and Eve were before they first sinned–that is, before they no longer believed God about their perfection.

The first sin wasn't eating a piece of fruit, it was believing they'd have discernment over their identity–apart from God. Many of today's churches do the same thing. Refusing to focus on and teach the truth of who we are, instead, behavior discernment for identity is their fixation. As a result, countless well-behaved non-saved people follow suit.

Jesus didn't come to clothe our nakedness with stuff to do or stuff to stop. Again, those are fig leaves advertised by religion and those who find their worth in conduct and sentiment. Jesus came to give you a new life, *His* life (see Colossians 3:4, John 3:16, 14:6). He came to give you His very own righteousness by way of being spiritually killed off, and spiritually reborn! Once reborn, you can't be unborn! Spiritual birth into God's family is final! (See John 1:12, 3:6,7, 2 Corinthians 5:17-21, Colossians 1:22,3:3, 1 John 4:17, Romans 6:6,7,18, Galatians 2:20, Ephesians 1:5).

From *that* free righteousness, by way of birth, we live! We aren't putting religious stuff on to *be* righteous, we *are* righteous!

An identity-confused person might yell at me, "Yeah, hate the sin love the sinner!"

No. Don't even hate the sin. Hating sin is a distraction from focusing on our righteousness. It also takes our thoughts off of the righteousness available for spiritually dead people, unbelievers. Hating the sin of others is what the Pharisees did, the nemeses of our Savior. Christ Himself isn't even focused on hating our unnatural actions and attitudes as a saints (see John 3:17); and further, Christians are *not* sinners. We *were* sinners.

"Wrong, Matt! Even Paul called himself the chief of sinners!"

Friend, Paul was speaking in past tense when he said this. Go read the entire passage and you'll discover he was using his old life *as* a sinner (because he lived by the Mosaic Law and persecuted Christians) as his best example of God's mercy (see 1 Timothy 1:12-16). Paul never called Christians "sinners" in any of his letters. His goal was to constantly remind them of their *past* cleansing, their rebirth, and new life as adopted children of God–never calling them sinners, constantly calling them saints (see Romans 1:7, Ephesians 1:1, 1 Corinthians 1:2, 2 Corinthians 1:1, Colossians 1:2, 1 Thessalonians 3:13, 2 Thessalonians 1:10).

We are holy people who sometimes don't *act* holy. Just the same as an eagle "could" be seen pecking on the ground with chickens, such an act would never make that eagle a yardbird. It was *born* regal. It will always *be* regal. Same with you, Christian. Sinful acts or thoughts won't cause you to become sinful, they just won't make any sense or feel right permanently. Do you want proof you're saved? Try sinning. Denial will only last so long, soon enough, you *know* you weren't made for that. Why is this? Because from the moment you first believed, you were remade *sinless*. Living a holy life is the most natural thing you could possibly do! (See Romans 6:6,7, 2 Corinthians 5:17, Colossians 1:22, Galatians 2:20, 1 Peter 1:15:16).

So today, my friends, know this: Don't be distracted with the original temptation of man–knowing good from evil. Instead, be led by God's Spirit. He will never lead you into evil, so don't worry. Satan will try to do this, as will self-centered people; unrenewed thoughts and the power of sin will too. But the Holy Spirit of Jesus Christ came to educate you on the truth of who you really are *after* you believe He's forgiven you. You are good! You are holy! You are blameless and complete!

A prayer for you: *Dad, today I want to thank you for replacing untruths with truths, in my mind. For so long, you and I both know I was obsessed with NOT doing evil things. As a result evil things were rampant. You didn't want that. You wanted me to just live my life, and when I made a mistake, recognize it and move forward. Through this freedom, you've taken me from having a heavily-burdened sin-consciousness, to a mindset of free-flowing righteousness! IT FEELS SO GOOD AND I'M GRATEFUL! Right now, I lift up all who are reading this, directly to you. So many are focused on the knowledge of good and evil, and you want to set them free. Yes, there is a such thing as good and evil, but you're taking care of that. Remove this burden from their thinking and teach them that's not their*

job. Help them to start focusing on identity instead of behavior, because authentic righteous behavior can only be produced through understanding our true right-standing identity. As they do, like me, they'll feel as if a huge weight has been lifted! This is your Spirit setting them free in their minds! As believers in Christ, their spirit is already free, but KNOWING THIS is what makes the difference in enjoying our lives! In Jesus' name I pray, amen.

Day 22

The Truth About 1 John 1:9 and James 5:16

"If we confess our sins, he is faithful and just to forgive us our sins and to cleanse us from all unrighteousness."

1 John 1:9

"Here, take it," a Jewish man says with his head hung low, passing off his prized goat to the priest. From the tribe of Levi, the priest walks the goat back behind the curtain in the temple, to be sacrificed for the past *year* of this man's sins. Of course, this was before Jesus was sacrificed for *all* of mankind's sins–but still, this was how the Jews received *annual* forgiveness from God. Not sin by sin, not day by day, not week by week. Instead, 365 days of atonement for every sin committed, once a year.

They didn't ask, hope, plead, or beg for forgiveness. They didn't repent for forgiveness, nor did they negotiate, get baptized, walk an isle, make alms or confess. The Hebrew people were confident as they passed off an animal as payment for sins *one time* every year. They didn't worry about their sins being forgiven, until the following year, because they knew they couldn't do anything about them until the *next* Day of Atonement (see Leviticus 16 and 23, Hebrews 9 and 10).

Jesus was a Jew, John was a Jew, Peter, James, Paul–every disciple was a Jew. They all knew the only way to be forgiven was annually by way of blood. The words "ask for forgiveness" are not in the Bible for a reason. Asking never forgave anyone. Blood had to be shed and it was faith in that blood's ability *to* forgive–because it was presented to God–which truly forgave (Hebrews 10:8).

A Jewish man or woman's act of faith in presenting blood *to* God *for* their transgressions–breaking one or more of 613 commandments–is *what* settled them up with our Creator. There was nothing special about a bull or sheep's hemoglobin, it was the heart of the person giving it to the priest that mattered (see Hebrews 11, Romans 3:21,22, Galatians 2:16).

Jesus said, "It is finished!" as He allowed Himself to be sacrificed on the Cross. These words would immediately resonate with the Jewish people; an explosion of epiphanies for all who would believe in what just happened: the Day of Atonement was abolished through <u>His</u> blood (see John 19:30, Matthew 27:51, Hebrews 8:13, 10:26-29).

The yearly cycle of slaughter for the Jews was a shadow of what Christ would do *once* and for all time! No more annual treks! No more animal sacrifices! Just faith in *one* Sacrifice! They were finally free from such a heavy burden!

Fast forward to today. The modern church has turned *confession* into a bar of soap for believers in Christ. From the get-go, this makes no sense because confession never forgave the Jews according to Moses, so it definitely doesn't forgive us according to the New Covenant. If this were the case, I'd rather be living by the Old Covenant because they received forgiveness all at once–yearly. Further, there's not a single Old Testament verse which claims confession resulted in God forgiving someone once and for all time. God requires *blood* to forgive, not words.

Something else that's very important to know is this: animal blood didn't *remove* sins, Jesus' blood *did*. Instead, it atoned for or "covered up" sins, bringing their account back to zero. If a Hebrew man or woman had a boom-box, "Back In Black" would've been blaring from the speakers as they walked away from the temple–feeling relief until the next year. Just look:

> *"In fact, the Law requires that nearly everything be cleansed with blood,*
> *and <u>without the shedding of blood there is no forgiveness</u>."*
> *(Hebrews 9:22)*

> *"But those sacrifices are <u>an annual reminder of sins</u>. It is <u>impossible</u> for*
> *the blood of bulls and goats to <u>take away sins</u>." (Hebrews 10:3,4)*

Animal blood *reminded* them of sins, Jesus took *away* sins, for all who would believe! John the Baptist expressed this truth the moment he first laid eyes on Christ:

> *The next day he saw Jesus coming toward him, and said, "Behold, the*
> <u>*Lamb*</u> *of God, who <u>takes away</u> the sin of the world! (John 1:29)*

Why would he call Jesus a *Lamb*, a proper noun? Because lamb blood forgave and Christ was the last (and only) Sacrifice *from* God *to* God! Jesus was the most perfect Sacrifice ever, resulting in no need for any further killings by priests! (See Hebrews 10:26-29). Messiah was a gift to us *for* our sins–to pay them off permanently–so we can live in graceful freedom while no longer worrying about punishment from our Creator! (See John 3:16-18, 8:36, 1 John 3:5, 2:2, Galatians 5:1, Romans 5:1, Ephesians 2:8,9, 1 John 4:18).

John the Baptist was a Jew too, so he was looking forward to the day he'd no longer have to make a trip to get forgiveness at the Day of Atonement.

The Holy Spirit revealed that this man walking toward him would do just that! (See John 1:17,29). Yet still, we Christians are confused about how forgiveness is received. We've been taught the error of "confession to be forgiven" when only faith in Jesus forgives us *once* (see Hebrews 10:10, Romans 6:10).

As a believer, it's impossible to be more forgiven than we are at this very moment. As an unbeliever, it's impossible to be any less forgiven. Confession doesn't achieve forgiveness for either person, repeatedly. On purpose or not, distorted context of Scripture is to blame for this fallacy. There are only two verses in the New Testament which speak of confession of sin–1 John 1:9 and James 5:16–and *neither* have to do with continual forgiveness from God.

Before I continue, if you believe confession forgives *you* on a regular basis, ask yourself this: *"What if I forget to confess a sin?"*

God doesn't forget. Just because we allow a sin to float away into the rear-view mirror of our life *without* confessing it, that doesn't mean it's no longer a sin. Our memory, or incorrectly justifying a sin, doesn't save us or keep us saved. All sins are willful and all sins must be dealt with by Christ's blood. Do you believe He has the power to remove *every* sin–past, present, and future?

Friend, the answer is yes. Yes, He does. All of our sins were in the future when He died for them. He isn't bound by time. We are. He temporarily joined us in our *human* time frame, but only to take care of our sin problem with the Father. Then off He went, back into the timeless realm, leaving us His Spirit for comfort, strength, and guidance (see John 1:14, 14:18,26, 8:58, Revelation 22:13, 2 Peter 3:8, 1 John 2:2).

Please ask yourself one more question if you're focused on confessing: *"Why not just do a blanket confession for all of my sins for my entire life and get it over with?"*

Seems shallow, doesn't it? That's not much of a relationship, is it? This theology makes no sense for a reason: because it's not true.

Let's break down 1 John 1:9 so we can be free in our thinking and truly enjoy our union with Christ!

"If we confess our sins, he is faithful and just to forgive us our sins and to cleanse us from all unrighteousness." (1 John 1:9)

I opened up this devotional explaining how the Jews were forgiven. Also known as Israel, this people group was God's original chosen community to have a relationship with Him through the Old Covenant brought in by Moses. God *requires* Covenants. This is important because if we don't understand how God forgives, this single verse can easily make us think admitting our mistakes regularly *keeps* us forgiven. However, the first chapter of 1 John is an invitation *to* believe *from* those who walked with Christ. John is making an appeal to unbelievers who said Jesus never came in the flesh, and that "sin" was a made-up idea. Just start from the beginning and you'll see.

But if you simply look at the verse *before* this one–1 John 1:8–the context is straightforward. John is addressing people who believed they had *never* sinned a day in their lives; as if sin was not a real thing:

"If we claim to be <u>without</u> sin, we deceive ourselves and the truth is not in us." (1 John 1:8)

This is a solicitation for non-believers to *admit* their sinfulness, which is the first step to becoming a Christian. What happens after we confess, after we agree with God, "Yeah, I am sinful. I need to be forgiven by Jesus."? The next verse answers that. He is faithful and just to forgive us our sins and to cleanse us from *all* unrighteousness–ALL. The original Greek word, *ola*, means all. There is no ambiguity of how much forgiveness we receive the moment we first admit our sinfulness. After we do, we are cleansed by being supernaturally killed, resurrected, and then *combined* with Christ–while still *in* these bodies! (See Romans 6:6,7, Galatians 2:20, 2 Corinthians 5:17, 1 Corinthians 6:17,19).

Does He cleanse our sinful behaviors and attitudes? No. But He cleanses *us*. From this new identity our behaviors and attitudes can become authentically holy because *now* we have the heart of God in our very being (see Ezekiel 36:26, Hebrews 10:16, Romans 6:17, 1 Corinthians 6:11). There's no need to fake it 'til we make it. Living right is what we do naturally (see 2 Peter 1:4).

Confession doesn't keep straightening out a crooked stick, we're no longer catawampus. The Cross has completely ironed our spirit out!

Friend, this verse has nothing to do with confessing daily, weekly, tri-annually, or whenever our conscience is killing us; and it definitely has nothing to do with confessing to a priest. With all due respect, priests are a made-up, modern day, useless middle man. That collar means nothing according to the New Covenant. There's not one New Testament verse claiming we need a priest for anything.

On this side of the Cross, priests are obsolete, but even back then, nobody confessed anything to them to be forgiven. They were simply agents. Just like today, no more holy than anyone else. In fact, they had to offer animals for their *own* sins *before* they could do this for others. The priests at the temple–from the tribe of Levi, descendants of Aaron–took the animals from non-Levites as the second baton holder. If you weren't from the Levitical priesthood you weren't allowed to go behind the curtain where sacrifices were made on the altar. You had to wait outside. Now, there's only *one* mediator between God and man, it's Christ. He entered the real temple in heaven, once, and He's not doing it ever again. New Covenant priestly representation isn't biblical at all. The truth is, every believer becomes a part of a royal priesthood! (See Hebrews 1:3, 4:16, 5:3, 9:7, 11, 12, 1 Timothy 2:5, 1 Peter 2:9).

James said we all stumble in many ways (see James 3:2). Because of this, he advises us to confess our sins to one another (see James 5:16). This is the only other verse about confessing sins in the New Testament. Which begs the question: If confession was necessary to be repeatedly forgiven, don't you think Paul or Peter would have mentioned it at least once?

I sure do.

Let's dive deeper into this passage from Jesus' brother, James:

"Therefore confess your sins to each other and pray for each other so that you may be healed. The prayer of a righteous person is powerful and effective." (James 5:16)

First of all, who is righteous? Every Christian, equally (see 2 Corinthians 5:21, Colossians 1:22, Acts 10:34). We aren't going to higher "levels" of well-behaved religious people *so that* we can be healed. This verse is *de*-scriptive not *pre*-scriptive, and it's referring to any believer in Jesus Christ, not just church leaders.

We could ask absolutely anyone to pray for us, and if they're a Christian, their prayers are just as powerful and effective as anyone's. But let's back up. Why would I confess my sins to someone else?...So I can be *prayed for*, so I can receive healing *in my mind*. So that I can get *whatever* off my chest.

This isn't talking about physical healing because St. Jude's would be empty. This isn't talking about spiritual healing because the Cross would be useless. This is talking about our mindsets.

If I'm struggling with a sin, I always feel better when I reach out to a trusted friend and say, "Hey buddy, I need you to pray for me. This is what I'm going through right now." It's a very healing thing. However, their prayers are *not* causing me to be forgiven. Only my one-time belief in Christ's forgiveness did such a thing.

The advice and counsel of someone isn't repeatedly forgiving me. It didn't forgive the Jews according to the Old Covenant, and it's not neurotically forgiving *us* now. We are free to confess to dependable friends and family, and we are free to confess to God. We should do this each time the Holy Spirit leads us to.

Confession simply means *admitting* or *agreeing with*. It's a very healthy thing! Confession reveals God's truths and your identity! Confession will ease your mind!

So today, my friends, know this: Confess away! 1 John 1:9 and James 5:16 are true! If you've never confessed to a loved one about a struggle, try it out. It works wonders in your thought life. Even more importantly, if you've never confessed your need to be cleansed of your sins once and for all time, do it now! Today is your day of salvation! Afterwards, know that you *have been* cleansed of *all* unrighteousness! You are now sinless and free!

A prayer for you: *Father, today I want to thank you for once for all forgiveness. What a wonderful idea. What a GRACEFUL idea. We have it so good as New Covenant believers, much better than any patriarch or prophet of the Old! We've been forgiven by grace through faith in Jesus, ONE TIME. Amazing! Right now, I lift up all who are reading this, directly to you. So many of them have been taught the error of confession to be constantly forgiven, yet this is not from you. Such an idea creates confusion and fear, removing the potency of the Cross in their minds. It also causes self-righteousness, belittlement of sinful actions and attitudes, hiding, covering up, and hypocrisy. Set them free, Father. Reveal the truth! You forgive us in full from the moment we first believe we NEED to be forgiven by your Son! What an awesome gift! Keep teaching us more about what He's done FOR us and TO us! Amen.*

Day 23

Debunking Christian Myths Part 3

"What is truth?" Pilate asked.

See John 18:38

Jesus said the truth will set us free (see John 8:32). So if the truth sets us *free* then error keeps us bound, shackled, and imprisoned. Allowing us to live a life of lies, as a Christian, is not what Christ came to do. He has no desire for us to fake our holiness. We *are* holy, so we should live holy.

Jesus came so we can enjoy absolute liberty, not a quasi-gospel of liberty plus bondage. Paul explains this truth to the Galatians who had forgotten what Christ had done:

> *"It is for freedom that Christ has set us free. Stand firm, then, and do not let yourselves be burdened <u>again</u> by a yoke of slavery." (Galatians 5:1)*

There's a lot of good things going on in this particular verse, but I've underlined *again*. Again means *returning to the same thing*. Why would Paul advise them to not become slaves *again*? Because they were trying to justify themselves through Mosaic Law observance, again, 613 all-or-nothing commandments. Read the two previous chapters and it's simple to see.

Paul is not referring to drinking, smoking, sleeping around, cursing, and skipping church. He's chastising Christians who were trying to be religious; Christians attempting to *add to* what Christ has already completed: 600+ Thou Shalts, which included the Ten Commandments (see Deuteronomy 4:2).

The people in Galatia had become bored with the message and simplicity of the gospel. They wanted to have their ears tickled by being told, "Doing more religious stuff will increase your right-standing with God." Paul called them fools for doing such a thing (see Galatians 3:1). If legalism was now their focus, their mindsets had fallen *away* from grace (see Galatians 5:4). Had they lost their salvation? No. Grace would never allow that to happen because then grace would no longer be grace. *But* their purposefulness would be put on pause (see Galatians 2:16, Romans 11:6, Revelation 2:4).

Lots of Christians fall away from grace *in their thinking*. Behavior-centered teaching is to blame. A double-talk mix of, "Come to Jesus just as you are, and be completely forgiven," then the next week, "Sinner! There's no hotter place in hell than for a backslider like you!"

This slave-causing theology of, "You're saved by grace through faith, until you sin again," has warped the mindsets of countless believers–not their eternal security–but their thought life. Enjoying freedom is not on their radar of faith. Rules and regulations are the blips, while overbearing, cliquey, charismatic people throw commands out like Skittles. Emotionalism sells the tithe, so certain preachers make sure the seats are full of fans and groupies, teacher's pets, or petrified sheep.

If you have legitimate questions, you're no longer welcome. Fall in line, eat what you're fed, or shut up and leave.

But why? Why can't we just stick to the freedom of the gospel? Innocently, many Christian leaders just don't understand the New Covenant and the power of the Cross. Instead, they rely on their good looks, smooth talk, intelligence, fear-mongering, church size (big *or* small), collar, or supposed spiritual gifts. Pressure is their message of choice. Even when their teachings *begin* graceful, rarely do they end that way. A call to action is always their M.O.–falling away from grace yet again.

To make matters worse, behavior repentance hounding has been handed down from previous generations, there's a lot to unlearn. We've been taught to focus on the pay-out and not the nourishing of the product. This is why a lot of well-behaved churchgoers will be in hell. They thought "what they do" is what saves. It does not (see Matthew 7:21-23).

The word "repent" in the Bible means "change of belief" more often than "change of behavior." After all, the Jews were the most obedient people on the planet. If *actions* is what made a person right with God, why would *they* need to repent of what they were doing? It was the heathen Gentiles who didn't know how to live righteously, not them.

Behavior repentance for salvation makes no sense for a reason: sin modification and sin management is not the truest meaning of repent, especially in the gospels and in Acts.

Self-absorbed people have twisted Scripture attempting to *appear* more holy than others, and we've believed it. Holiness is impossible to earn or sustain through behavior change. Authentic holiness only comes by way of identity. It's *us* who has made the word repent into a law, into a *work*. Paul rebukes the Romans over this topic:

> *"And if by grace, then it <u>cannot be based on works</u>; if it were, <u>grace would no longer be grace</u>." (Romans 11:6)*

When it comes to stirring up the power of sin in a human being, made-up laws of behavior repentance are just as lethal as Mosaic laws (see Romans

7:8). Therefore, we must count ourselves dead to anything which would cause us to *think* we will be punished by God. Christians will never be punished by God for a *single* mess up, a *single* sin. This includes sins of omission and commission (see Romans 5:1, 1 John 2:2, 4:18).

Authentic ambassadors of Christ will teach you *freedom* and that you are completely reconciled with God through faith (see John 8:32, 2 Corinthians 5:11-21). Don't worry, the Holy Spirit will never lead you into a life of sin or licentiousness. The self-centered people think freedom gives us a license to sin, but that's only because they find *their* value in "amazing" behavior, which, like the Pharisees, is laughable (see Galatians 2:21). *This* is the exact mindset which must be repented of in order to be saved–the mindset of "whitewashed tombs" (see Matthew 23:27-28).

If you're dealing with two-faced messages which create church hierarchies, as well as constant "Be like me!" teachings, please understand those are chains. Those things are *not* giving you freedom. Further, the sermons of, "God has done *so* much for you! The *least* you can do is pay Him back!" *that* is bondage too. It's error.

The truth is, we could never pay God back and He doesn't expect us to. How could we possibly do such a thing? How could *we* pay back the Omniscient One? God is not needy! (See Acts 17:25). He's making this planet float and spin in the middle of nothing. He's holding us at just the right distance from the sun to give us light and warmth *without* burning or blinding us. He's providing oxygen for your blood as you read this sentence. The rhythm of your heartbeat is ticking by *His* choice and desire–nothing is making it beat but Him.

GOD. NEEDS. NOTHING. Instead, He *wants* a relationship with us. Our relationship is not payment, it's our purpose. Trying to pay God back is one of the most shackling teachings on the market. Don't fall for it. *You* can't do this–neither can I–and that's okay because our Dad just wants to be our Dad.

Please, don't get angry at teachers, relatives, and friends–or anyone–about this type of teaching. Learn from my mistakes and don't attack because you'll regret it. Simply stay anchored in His love, the love infused with your spirit. Then express this love to those who don't understand it–toward confused church leaders. I'm not even saying leave a church such as this. I'm saying, know the truth.

When we know the truth the truth will set us free *in our minds*. As Christians, our spirits are already free, but do we *know* that? This is part 3 of my "Debunking Christian Myths" devotionals. If you'd like to read part 1 and 2, they're available in my book series, *60 Days for Jesus*, as well as on my website.

I pray that what I've just written has helped you understand your freedom in Christ better. Here are three additional myths:

1. **You can't get any closer to God than you currently are at this very moment in time.** Why is this so important to know? Because as a Christian your actions and attitudes cannot change your union with Christ. The Bible says you are *hidden* inside of God (see Colossians 3:3). It says you are one *with* the Spirit of Jesus (see 1 Corinthians 6:17). It says your body is *His* temple (see 1 Corinthians 6:19). You can't get any closer than that! Let's look at it this way: God is milk, you are cereal. When you put milk in cereal the milk becomes one with the cereal, and the cereal becomes one with the milk–still separate–yet now, both are *inside* of each other. The same thing happened with you and God from the *moment* you first believed Jesus forgave you! Your old spirit died, it was resurrected *with* Jesus, and then *united* with Him permanently (see Romans 6:6,7). The only thing that could cause this relationship to dissolve is if Jesus dies again–and that ain't happening! (see Hebrews 7:25, John 14:19). You were supernaturally reborn *connected* to Him. You can't "walk away" from being born, nor

can anything you do or not do make you *unborn*. Birth is final! (See John 1:12, 3:6,7). Sure, you can get closer to God in your *thinking*, but not in your identity. Friend, if you honestly believe that what you're doing and not doing is causing you to be close, then far, close, then far, how can you be sure?...You can't. If you're not sure, then it's error. If it's error, then it's not freeing, so it's not the truth.

2. **Christians won't be judged for "every idle word we speak."** Context is key to deciphering this myth. In Matthew 12:36, Jesus said, *"And I tell you this, you must give an account on judgment day for every idle word you speak."* However, upon deeper review, Jesus is chewing out the legalistic religious people who didn't believe in Him. Just start up in verse 22 and read down. He isn't talking to believers, but Pharisees. Christ had just removed a demon from a man and these behavior-focused vultures said He did so by way of Satan. In return, He called them evil and a bunch of snakes. *Then* Jesus said *they* would have to give an account for their careless words. As much as this will disarm a person who struggles with legalanity, this is *not* for Christians. Just think about it. What are careless words according to God? Sins. What would happen if we were judged for a *single* sin? Death (see Romans 6:23). What did Jesus do? He died! His death was enough! (See Hebrews 1:3, 10:10). Sins of idle words will not "sneak in" on our Judgment Day. That is religious garbage. This is something a Pharisee would claim because *they* think they've "sinned less" and "God grades on a curve"–He doesn't. God requires perfection (see Matthew 5:48). As a matter of fact, Christ Himself said we will not be judged for *any* sin: "Whoever hears my word and believes him who sent me has eternal life and <u>will not be judged</u> but has crossed over from death to life" (see John 5:24). It can't be both, and it won't be both. The Cross was a huge success!

3. **Christians don't have sinful hearts.** I was listening to a podcast the other day and the person said, "We have sinful hearts," then in the next breath, "We shouldn't sin." Well that makes no sense at all. If we have sinful hearts then sinning should be *exactly* what we should be doing. Sinning would be natural. If we truly have sinful hearts, why deny ourselves? I mean, if our identity is sinful, why not just sin? Do you see the double-talk? The bondage? The truth of the gospel is we got a new heart, a sinless heart, a heart just like God's! (See Hebrews 8:10, Ezekiel 36:26). Now *this* is why we shouldn't sin! Our heart is our spirit–it's *who* we are. Yes, the word "heart" can be used in a different way *other* than describing our spirit–such as "all that we are." But for context, and according to Scripture, our heart is our spirit. The grace-confused people will claim we have a sinful heart–a wicked heart–but that was according to the Old Covenant. The Prophet Jeremiah was explaining the human heart condition from birth (see Jeremiah 17:9). This was *before* Christ came and gave us the ability to be supernaturally crucified with Him, by way of faith, which allowed Him to give us a new heart, and then *join* our heart (see Romans 6:6,7, Galatians 2:20, 2 Corinthians 5:17, 1 Corinthians 6:17,19, Ephesians 2:8,9). If we still had wicked hearts He wouldn't be able to make His home *in* us. It would be just like the Old Covenant, His Spirit coming and going based on actions, attitudes, and divine appointments. God's Spirit cannot live in wicked, sinful places. This is why we are just as holy as He is and our hearts are sinless! (See Colossians 1:22, 1 John 4:17).

So today, my friends, know this: You are free, so live free! You are as close to God as you can possibly get! Christ has removed the punishment for all of our sins, even the careless stuff we sometimes say. But most of all, I want you to know your heart is good. It's not sinful. It's not wicked. As a believer, our minds are still catching up to this truth, our actions and attitudes are too–but our identity is not! Our identity is final and we are complete! (See Colossians 2:10).

A prayer for you: *Heavenly Father, today I want to thank you for freedom; freedom from sin, freedom from hell, freedom from living a life in confusion. These freedoms come by way of your grace. It is when we truly allow ourselves to bask in the richness of your grace, we enjoy the abundant life of Christ! Right now, I lift up all who are reading this, directly to you. Dad, I know some of the things they've just read might seem scary. Your grace is a scary thing when we've been taught error for so long. But without your grace, life is even more scary, because the pressure is all on us. Take the pressure off them, Father. Your grace is infinitely loving, and your infinite love casts out all fear because fear has to do with punishment. Jesus was punished FOR us, for every sin we'd ever commit, so we don't have to be afraid! Teach us more each day and take us deeper into what all He's done! Thank you for freedom! Amen.*

Day 24

Confessions of a Hungover Saint

*"And that is what some of you were. But
you were washed, you were sanctified, you
were justified in the name of the Lord Jesus
Christ and by the Spirit of our God."*

1 Corinthians 6:11

Saturday morning hangovers used to ruin my entire weekend. What started out as a way to relax and have fun on Friday, nine out of ten times, got out of control. It didn't matter if my Friday evening consisted of meeting up with some friends for dinner at a local restaurant, or drinking at home, I could never figure out how to drink normally. You know? Like two or three beers and be done?

"What is *wrong* with me?" was a regular Saturday morning statement I said in self-pity as I once again had to lay on the couch all day because of the pain. Sometimes I'd fake it and go do stuff on Saturday, but the physical and mental agony was real. I had even gotten to the point where I gauged my hangovers:

1. "I'm not *really* hungover."
2. "I'm not drinking the rest of the weekend."
3. "I'm never drinking again. I need to get some help."

This insane cycle continued until I was 32 years old. I'm 37 now, and all along what I *should* have been asking myself—rather than "What's wrong with me?"—is "What's *right* with me?"

Now *this* is the question God really wanted me to be answering! The truth was, yes, my alcoholic actions and attitudes *were* wrong, but *I* was right in every way. My identity, that is. How can I be so bold to say such a thing?... Because God said it, and God cannot lie. He doesn't half-way remake us, we become complete from the moment we receive Christ (see Colossians 2:9,10). We *receive* Christ, by grace, through faith, once (see Ephesians 2:8,9, Hebrews 10:10).

The self-righteous folk who are centered on behavior can't fathom this. They cannot compute that God would be so brash as to make us holy by birth, rather than by bodily movements and geographic positioning. They, like the Pharisees, without Christ in their reborn spirit, won't make it into eternity with us who are sanctified in full (see Matthew 7:21-23, 1 Corinthians 6:11,17).

Even though I struggled with this particular sin, alcoholism, *I* was not sinful. Me. My identity. I did not know this because of the lies of supposed Bible teachers. They had twisted the Scripture to their liking, for their Christian country clubs, without expressing the truth of what Jesus really does to a person's spirit *instantly* by faith. Which is recreates them, then makes His home in them (see Romans 6:6-10, John 14:20, Colossians 3:3).

I was taught to shape up or ship out. Fury and resentment flooded my mind because of such. I could never be good enough and they made that clear. They commingled what I did with who I was, while sanctimoniously doing the same for themselves. When I finally found out the truth, that I had been perfectly cleansed forever since I first believed, I was ultra-mad at them (see Hebrews 10:14). But over time, the Spirit taught me to forgive them because forgiveness is a natural thing for a saint–and that is what I am. That is what *every* Christian is, equally. Even them, if they believed at some point or another.

The same grace they were against–or refused to teach clearly by mixing in behavior repentance in order to achieve and sustain–*Christ* was teaching me I had to hand out *to* them. Talk about an explosion in my mind. But, after that atomic bomb went off, *peace* flooded my thinking. They needed to experience God's grace from *me*. So *I* needed to begin thinking of quasi-grace teachers with the same love that Christ thinks of me with, genuinely. I'm still learning how to do this and Jesus is walking with me, teaching me day by day.

"Matthew, don't attack. Don't belittle. Don't criticize. Show them grace because I love them too."

"Okay. Help me. *Please*. Do this *through* me."

The truth was, from the moment I first believed in His forgiveness as a young boy, my spirit immediately died in the spiritual realm. It was crucified, buried, and resurrected *with* Jesus—connected to Him for good—never to be undone by my unholy choices or mindsets! I had inherited as a free gift *His* own righteousness! (See Romans 5:17, 6:6-10, Galatians 2:20, 2 Corinthians 5:17,21).

This new spirit of mine, the spirit I received in the 80's, was and is holy, blameless, and complete! It is reborn *of* God, never to go back to *not* being His child because birth is final! We cannot sin our way out of being born! We cannot turn our *back* on being born! Neither can we "un-believe" we've been born! So, unchangeable holiness is what we have to deal with *rather* than the fear of no longer being a child of God! (See Colossians 1:22, 2:9,10, John 1:12, 3:6,7, 2 Timothy 2:13).

…Getting drunk all the time would never feel right to me because I was a new creation who was not *made* to be controlled by a liquid. Truth be told, drinking was something the Spirit of Christ within me didn't *want* me to do at all. Sure, some people can have a few and be done, they can drink just as much as Jesus drank, but not me. God revealed this in my spirit, convincing me that I should never drink another drop—and I gotta tell ya, I wish I didn't wait so long. Life is good, even when it's tough. Why? Because worrying about alcohol or its effects on me is never something I have to deal with, ever. What a relief!

So today, my friends, know this: If this sounds like something you needed to hear today, don't wait any longer to begin living out your true self, saint. If you've believed Jesus forgave you, He did, once and for all time, and *you* are now a saint. You are a holy person, spotless and set apart from the world. Yes, *you*. I'm not referring to you with just a Jesus filter on, but *you*, yourself, you are good! You are a brand new, heaven-ready, self-controlled coheir with the Son of God! Now live *out* who you truly are on the inside! Live free, because that's what you are!

A prayer for you: *Dad, I feel so much JOY inside! When I think about what you've done, I want to type with exclamation points and all caps in every sentence! You sent your own Son here to die a death He didn't deserve so that I can live my life in the most abundant way possible! I AM FREEEEEEEEEE! Thank you! Thank you for new life! Thank you for teaching me that I HAD THIS LIFE ALL ALONG FROM WHEN I FIRST BELIEVED! It is YOU! It is YOUR SPIRIT IN ME!… But I must calm down for a moment. I want to pray for those who aren't enjoying*

the freedom you've given them. I've been there, and you know it. The enemy can blind us to who we really are, your kids. He sees our spirit, that it glows like Christ, so he lies to us ABOUT us. Sometimes he even uses Scripture, by taking it out of context. But, once we've placed our faith in Jesus as our Savior, we instantly become one with you. You remake us as sinless spirits, then join us. Teach them that, Father. Reveal the truth of what you've done to them. You've recreated them IN Christ. They are NOT addicted, they are free. Renew their addicted THINKING to this truth. Teach them that self-control IS within them. It's Jesus. Reveal the omnipotent power that lies within their hearts. Comfort them. Lift them up. Help them to grow in your grace and in confidence. Let them know you'll never leave them, no matter what they do or where they go. You're committed. You made this commitment at the Cross, and they've inherited the benefits by faith. Help them come to understand they've been reborn. Let them know they ARE free, and that they HAVE new life–YOUR life. In Jesus' name I pray, amen.

Day 25

Why It's Important to Protect
Your Eyes and Ears

"But blessed are your eyes because they see,
and your ears because they hear."

Matthew 13:16

"Let's find a new series to watch on Netflix together," my wife says to me as we relax on the couch one evening.

"Okay, that sounds good," I respond.

After scanning for a while, we decide on a new show.

It was a very interesting drama with a twist at the end each time–along with a cliffhanger–so you'd want to watch the next episode immediately. I really enjoyed the overall story, but, after binging several shows, it didn't sit right with me. The Holy Spirit was letting me know I shouldn't be watching it. This program was full of extremely foul language, sex, adultery, and lot of other things I should *not* be filling up my soul with.

The next morning I told Jennifer how I felt, and what I thought God was saying to me, and she said, "That's fine. We don't have to watch it."

To be clear, there was a time in my life when I wouldn't have allowed God to guide this type of decision. My old, unrenewed thinking, along with the enemy and the power of sin, didn't want me to *think* I was a prude.

"Don't be lame. It's no big deal. It's just a show on Netflix."

But this has nothing to do with being a goody-goody. On the contrary, it has everything to do with guarding my eyes and ears because both lead directly into my soul. My soul effects every aspect of my life, as well as the lives of those around me. What I pour into my soul will eventually come *out* through my hands, feet, mouth, and attitudes.

Jesus said, "Your eye is the lamp of your body. When your eyes are healthy, your whole body also is full of light. But when they are unhealthy, your body also is full of darkness" (Luke 11:34).

In context, Jesus is speaking about unbelief in Him—*that* is the truest form darkness. If you're a believer, you don't have darkness in you—in your spirit. Jesus cannot live in dark places. However, we can also look at this verse with the perspective of, "I need to protect my senses from things that do not match up with my spirit."

Don't get me wrong. I'm not saying shut everything off which is not of God. Paul told the Corinthians they'd have to go out of this world in order to do that (see 1 Corinthians 5:10). Instead, pay attention to your spirit's guidance as well as *the* Spirit's guidance. Both are holy, and both will sift out impediments (see Romans 6:6-10, Colossians 1:22, 1 Peter 1:16, Philippians 4:8).

You can't water a flower with motor oil and you can't feed your soul with trash. You must protect your soul at all times. You must be defensive about your mind, free will, and emotions, from *regular* outside sources. Not in a rude way, but in the same way as you express the gospel: with gentleness and respect (see 1 Peter 3:15).

The same goes for legalism and conservatism, both can be directly from hell. Because of poor teaching and centuries-old tradition, many Christians don't understand that we don't live under a single law or commandment of the Old Testament, including the Ten Commandments. The Old went away at the Cross *so that* the New could come in! The New is not an amendment, it's a whole new deal! It's the same God, but a *New* Covenant! (See Romans 10:4, Hebrews 8:6,13, 10:16).

"So Matt, are you saying we can just lie, cheat, and steal, and do whatever we want?!"

Friend, you, as a child of God, don't *want* to do those things because you've died to sin (see Romans 6:11). Just try any flavor of sin on for size and you'll see it doesn't fit. Sinning will never make sense to you *permanently* as a person who's been remade and then conjoined with Jesus' Spirit (see Galatians 2:20, 1 Corinthians 6:17).

One of the worst false teachings out there is that Christians like to sin–we don't. Sure, the flesh might get a flash-in-the-pan thrill from sin, but moments later, the real us sets off alarm bells. We don't *want* to do anything that isn't guided by the Holy Spirit. We truly want what God wants. Does God want to lie, cheat, and steal? No, and neither do you, and *you* don't want to be legalistic either.

"Then Matt, what do I *do*? How do I *know* what is right and wrong? I need a list!"

You really don't. Living by a list was Old Covenant, that's how Israel lived. Their list was "613 things to do and not do," ten of those things were the Ten Commandments. They always looked to this directory to define sin. Now, on this side of the Cross, *anything* that is not of faith is sin (see Romans 14:23).

"Anything that is not of faith is sin?! What does that mean?!"

It means anything you do or don't do, think or don't think, which is not led by Christ within you, is sin–but *you* are not sinful. You are a brand new sinless creation! (See 2 Corinthians 5:17).

"But Matt, what do I do! I need something to do!"

Okay. I'll give you something to do, but these two things will come naturally anyway as you just be yourself. Here they are:

1. Believe.
2. Love.

These are the two *new* commandments Jesus gave to us (John 13:34, 1 John 3:23). These two commandments are not added to Moses' 613–because the Bible says that list can't be modified (see Deuteronomy 4:2)–instead, they've replaced them. These commandments are not burdensome. 613 all-or-nothing *were*, and the Jews were ecstatic to get relief from that list (see 1 John 5:3, John 8:36, Matthew 11:28-30).

Legalistic teaching can lead a person to *think* they need a ton of stuff to do and not do. *Thinking* comes by way of what we allow to enter our eyes and ears. A *hint* of legalism causes us to never find rest, as we're constantly reaching out for the dangling carrot of impressing others and God (see Galatians 5:9).

Because of this, the grace-confused folk believe God comes and goes based on their performance. I hear Christians say all time, "I need Jesus!" but they already *have* Jesus. Behavior-focused sermons are to blame.

I also hear believers make the claim, "I gotta get closer to God!" But *inside* of God is as close as you can possibly can get, and that's where He's hidden every believer (see Colossians 3:3). Some say, "We need a revival!" But we don't need that either. Revival means *to come back to life*–yet, we've *done* that by accepting Christ's life as our own! (See Colossians 3:4, John 3:16).

What we need is our minds renewed to Him being 100% *in us*, teaching us gently, and that He'll never go away as long as He lives. We need to be taught more about who we already are, that way we can *mature* into who we already are (see Romans 12:2, Philippians 1:6, Galatians 5:22,23, Hebrews 7:25, John 14:26, 1 Corinthians 13:11).

Horrendous, legalistic, "You'll never be good enough!" tutoring enters our soul through our eyes and ears. Protect them at all costs! KNOW THE TRUTH! KNOW WHO YOU ARE! Christian, you are complete! You are lacking nothing! You have all you need for life and godliness! (See Colossians 2:9,10, 2 Peter 1:3).

Allow the Holy Spirit to guide you away from legalism in the same way He guides you away from watching porn, beating up your spouse, using the silent treatment, getting drunk all the time in front of your kids, or "innocently" flirting on social media. All of this stuff is damaging to your life's enjoyment. There is a better way, an authentic way. The way of a saint. That's what you are, believer.

So today, my friends, know this: It's important to protect your eyes and ears because both lead to your soul. Not your spirit–which is sealed up in perfection with Christ (see Ephesians 1:13)–but the customizable part of you. If it feels "off" then it probably is. The inspiration and motivation of the Holy Spirit of Christ will constantly guide you into peace, comfort, confidence, *love*, and sound mind. Let Him lead you more and more each day!

A prayer for you: *Dad, today I want to thank you for gently teaching me what I should and shouldn't be watching and listening to. I'm still learning, but I'm so much better off than I was. Keep guiding me with your Spirit. Right now, I lift up all who are reading this, directly to you. So many*

of these dear readers are struggling with discernment—what is and isn't of faith. Father, teach them how to be in this world but not of it. Jesus did this, so can we too! Help us to hear you more clearly every day! We know you'll do it! I pray all these things in Jesus' name, we love you, amen.

Day 26

The Truth About the Lord's Prayer

*"And when you pray, do not keep on babbling like
pagans, for they think they will be heard because
of their many words. Do not be like them, for your
Father knows what you need before you ask him."*

Matthew 6:7,8

The Lord's Prayer is something to behold. It's very interesting:

"Our Father in heaven,
hallowed be your name,
your kingdom come,
your will be done,
on earth as it is in heaven.
Give us today our daily bread.
And forgive us our debts,
as we also have forgiven our debtors.

And lead us not into temptation,
but deliver us from the evil one.

For if you forgive other people when they sin against you, your heavenly
Father will also forgive you. But if you do not forgive others their sins, your
Father will not forgive your sins." (Matthew 6:9-15)

First of all, the words *The Lord's Prayer* are not in the Bible. It is *us* who's put a label on this particular passage, found in Matthew 6. Yes, Jesus is the one praying it, but other than that fact, this is a prayer of death *if* we are truly respecting it. When we aren't holding this prayer to its true standard, we're watering down God's Word, cherry-picking here and there, or acting as if Jesus was not being serious. He *was* being serious. He came to fulfill the Law, not talk about it in hyperbole (see Matthew 5:17).

However, those who struggle with the tendency of legalism will fight tooth and nail to protect this prayer as they walk others through repeating it. But at the same time, *they* aren't doing it *in full* themselves–which is what God requires if you want to live by this prayer. That was Jesus' whole point.

If we back up into Matthew 5, Jesus says something that puts each person who "attempts" to live by this prayer on a flaming tightrope, high above a pool of starving crocodiles:

"Be perfect, therefore, as your heavenly Father is perfect."
(Matthew 5:48)

This statement by Christ caused the self-centered Jewish man or woman to think one of two things:

1. "Be perfect like God is perfect? How in the world am I supposed to do that? *Gulp*"
2. "This man needs to die. Who does he think he is?"

The *first* thought is what Jesus was wanting His listeners to have as He gave the Sermon on the Mount, as *well* as what we call the Lord's Prayer. Here's a rule of thumb when reading the gospels, which is Matthew, Mark, Luke, and John: If Jesus gives an impossible commandment or objective, that commandment or objective's purpose is to lead the listener toward faith in Him alone *apart* from what they do or do not do. His M.O. is to get people to free-fall into grace by creating "I *can't* do this" scenarios.

Let's look back into Matthew 5, one chapter before the Lord's Prayer, to see what the audience is supposed to be "doing perfectly," as well as the punishments for when they don't. Keep in mind, the Bible wasn't written in chapters. Chapters and verses were added much later by the publishers for easy searching. Therefore, Matthew 5 and 6 run together. Jesus–with a group of people who'd been taught the Law of Moses their entire life–*preaches* the Law. But then *increases* its difficulty in order to add on *top* of its current impossible standard:

1. You've been taught, do not murder. But I say don't even get angry or call anyone names. If you do, you will be in danger of hell (see Matthew 5:21,22).
2. Don't offer your animal sacrifice on the altar if someone has an issue with you–not *you*, but them. If *they* don't feel right about *you*, you can't get forgiveness at the Day of Atonement (see Matthew 5:23,24).
3. You've been taught, do not commit adultery. But I say don't even *think* about it. If you do, you are commanded to pluck out your eye. If your

hand sins, cut that off too. If you don't, you'll go to hell, but you'll have your eyes and hands (see Matthew 5:27-30).

4. If you divorce your wife except for sexual misconduct you brand *her* as the victim of adultery. Not just you, but her also, even though she did nothing wrong. Therefore, you're responsible for more than just *your* sins, but hers too, *and* the new man in her life (see Matthew 5:31,32).

5. Never swear by anything. If you do, Satan is speaking through you (see Matthew 5:33-37).

6. If someone hits you in the face, turn and let them hit you on the other side too. Never defend yourself (see Matthew 5:38-39).

7. If someone asks you for *anything,* give to them all they want and *never* ask them to pay you back (see Matthew 5:38-42).

After listing off all of these impossible-to-follow commandments, and increasing each's futility, He wanted to be sure His listeners *really* get it. So He throws down the gauntlet with the final touch, "Be perfect like God is perfect" (see Matthew 5:48).

But why? Why not just let the religious people live their lives and then God can give them their grade at the pearly gates? I mean, they weren't like those nasty Gentiles who had no hope with all that sinnin'. *They* were the original chosen people of our Creator to carry His oracles. So why, Jesus? Why buck-up against your own people?

…He was showing them a new way (see John 14:6). Those who were addicted to self-righteousness, distraught and shackled with behavior-focused theology? He was setting them free. He was showing them an easier way, and giving them a much lighter burden. He was offering green pastures of faith, rather than mountain-climbing of Law (see John 8:32, Psalm 23, Matthew 11:28-30).

In order to pull off this feat they had to die *to* the Law–that is, attempting to obey it–*so that* they could turn to faith in Him alone. Law and grace couldn't be mixed, they had to be separate (see Matthew 9:17). The Law hadn't died. It *still* hasn't died to this very day (see Matthew 5:17). But these new believers in Jesus had died to the Law, just like you and me, Christian.

Paul, a former devout Law-keeper, expresses this truth ad nauseam in his letters. Here are just *two* highlights:

"For through the Law I died to the Law so that I might live for God."
(Galatians 2:19)

"Therefore, my brothers, you also were made to die to the Law through the body of Christ, so that you might be joined to another, to Him who was raised from the dead, in order that we might bear fruit for God."
(Romans 7:4)

The *only* use of the Law–just like today–was to point out the dirt on peoples' faces. It never did anything to clean it off, especially by attempting to obey it (see Galatians 2:16, 3:11, Romans 3:20). Trying to become righteous by Mosaic Law observance–which included the Ten Commandments (see Deuteronomy 4:2, 2 Corinthians 3:7, Romans 7:8)–would be the same as me trying to become righteous by obeying the laws of my local city.

A cop will never pull me over and say, "You're doing a great job obeying the speed limit." No. The only time he'd pull me over is to correct me. Same with Moses' Law, and now the same with Jesus' *addition* to Moses' Law in Matthew 5 and 6.

This is *why* He gave the Sermon on the Mount, and this is *why* He prayed the Lord's Prayer! He was setting up the sanctimonious zealots for failure in order to herd them through the narrow gate of grace (see

Matthew 7:13, 14). But let's take a step back into the laundry list of Law in which Christ just spouted out, then added to, in order to make it even more difficult. Each time He upped the ante in Matthew 5, He first said, "You have heard *this*" and "You have heard *that*."

What was it they had heard?...The Mosaic Law! 613 commandments given to the Jews–who were also called *Israel*–the people group who followed Moses through the Red Sea *out* of slavery in Egypt. This is not written to us. *WE ARE GENTILES.* Non-Jewish people were never invited to *hear* the Sermon on the Mount or the Lord's Prayer. So when we attempt to retrofit this stuff into our faith, we've veered way off course. We have the Holy Spirit to guide us, not Moses (see 2 Corinthians 3:8, John 14:26, Galatians 5:22,23).

This is for the Hebrew people. *This* is their mail, not ours. We are simply spectators to *their* ballgame–not invited to play.

We were never given the Law which came by Moses. We only came to God through faith in Jesus Christ. Just look at the New Testament letters which were written *after* the Cross:

> "Here <u>there is no Gentile or Jew</u>, circumcised or uncircumcised, barbarian, Scythian, slave or free, <u>but Christ is all, and is in all</u>." *(Colossians 3:11)*

> "There is <u>neither Jew nor Gentile</u>, neither slave nor free, nor is there male and female, <u>for you are all one in Christ Jesus</u>." *(Galatians 3:28)*

So when we try to give the Sermon on the Mount our best shot, it's laughable. We must be perfect. This is *not* for us as New Covenant believers, which is the only Covenant available for both the Jew and Gentile (see Hebrews 8:6,13). Further, just because a person is Jewish that doesn't mean they will automatically get to go to heaven. They must repent of their unbelief in Christ as the Messiah in order to be saved (see Hebrews 10:26-29).

The Lord's Prayer isn't for us either. But for a moment, let's digress and say that it is. How about we break down each part of this prayer in order to open up our supernatural eyes to the truth? Christ is *not* encouraging the listeners, but chastising them by way *of* this prayer. The devout, pious folk–who thought God approved of them greatly–Jesus blasted away at:

1. **This prayer is for hypocrites.** He warms up this prayer, starting out in Matthew 6:5, by saying *don't* be like the hypocrites who pray this way. Even in verses 1-4, He's calling them out on their legalanity. I'm sure smoke was coming from the tops of their heads as Jesus declared that people who pray this way have *already* received their full reward. What reward was that? The admiration of those around them who *thought* they were holy–but really, they were not.

2. **This prayer is for show-offs.** In verse 6, He tells the legalists to go pray in a private room because He knew this would ruffle the feathers of their squawking egos. This is obviously not for Christians because we can pray anywhere we want, at any time we want, out loud or to ourselves. There is no law in prayer; there is no legislative red tape we must break through in order to talk to Dad. Romans 8:15 says we have the right to call God, *Abba*, which means *Daddy*. That's how close we are to Him. No need to go into a closet for a conversation, unless you want to.

3. **This prayer is for babblers.** Right before the supposed Lord's Prayer, in which everyone nowadays repeats, Jesus said *don't* repeat a prayer like this. Just look: *"And when you pray, <u>do not keep on babbling</u> like pagans, for they think they will be heard <u>because of their many words</u>"* *(Matthew 6:6)*. Pagans were non-Jews, us Gentiles, heathens. Just the same as people dancing around a campfire repeating the same prayer–thinking that babbling on and on will get God's attention–Jesus

scolded the Jews for this *same* action. Even today, the Jews who don't believe in Jesus as the Christ, those in limbo, they'll repeat the same prayers over and over at a giant wall in Jerusalem. There is no need for this. Say what you gotta say and be done.

4. **This prayer is for those who are not a part of the kingdom of God.** For verse 10, *"your kingdom come, your will be done, on earth as it is in heaven,"* the truth is God's kingdom *has* come and His will *has* been done *just* as it is in heaven. Jesus is speaking about Himself. His presence. The Jews who wanted God's kingdom to come were blind to the fact that their king was in front of them! They thought the Messiah would be a great warrior who would put the Jews back on top of the pecking order—*not* this kind carpenter from Nazareth. Jesus as the Messiah *is* God's will. Heaven was *in* the flesh, now on earth, walking and talking! The Jews needed to repent of their unbelief in this truth. They had no need to repent of poor behavior, as they were the most well-behaved people on the planet. They needed to turn *away* from Moses and *toward* Jesus! (See John 1:1-4,17, 6:40, Mark 1:15, Ephesians 2:6).

5. **This prayer is for those who don't have Christ living in them.** *"Give us today our daily bread"*—our daily bread *is* Jesus, so verse 11 *has been* fulfilled as well. We don't need God to keep giving us spiritual daily bread. Yes, our minds are being renewed day by day, but with Jesus in our spirit, we are no longer supernaturally hungry. By faith, our spirit has consumed the entirety of Christ's Spirit, once and for all time. We are *stuffed* (see John 6:35, Matthew 26:26, 1 Corinthians 6:17,19, Hebrews 10:10, Ephesians 1:6, 2:8,9, Romans 12:2, Revelation 7:6).

6. **This prayer is for those who are not forgiven.** *"Forgive us our debts as WE forgive our debtors?"* (See verse 12). This doesn't sound like good news to me, which is what "the gospel" means. What if I have a hint of unforgiveness in my mind? What if I've been hurt so badly I don't *feel*

like I've forgiven–even though I've chosen to? Friend, this is *not* New Covenant forgiveness, but forgiveness according to the Law. On this side of Calvary we forgive others *as* Christ has forgiven us, not to *get* forgiveness. If that were the truth, we'd all be doomed because Jesus said we must be perfect like God is perfect, and only *He* can forgive perfectly (see Colossians 3:13, Ephesians 4:32, Hebrews 1:3).

7. **This prayer is for those who are tempted to be legalistic.** *"Lead us not into temptation?"* (See verse 13). Temptation of what? *Breaking the Law of Moses.* Why would I say that? Because Jesus was *teaching* the Law of Moses in this passage, Matthew 5 and 6. What else could it possibly be? Random temptations? No. Temptations lead to sin. Sin was *defined* by Moses' Rolodex of 613 Thou Shalts.

8. **This prayer is for those who *could* have demons in them.** *"Deliver us from the evil one?"* (See verse 13) JESUS DID THIS IN FULL, AT THE CROSS! *"The reason the Son of God appeared was to destroy the devil's work"* (see 1 John 3:8). Christians cannot have a demon possess them. We are literally possessed by Christ's Spirit and He won't share us! (See 1 John 5:18, 1 Corinthians 6:19).

9. **This prayer is for those who don't understand New Covenant forgiveness.** God does not forgive us because we forgive others (see verses 14 and 15). He *forgave* us because we've believed Jesus *has* forgiven us (see John 3:16, 1 John 1:9, Romans 8:1, Hebrews 10:10). Most people who recite the Lord's Prayer won't finish this last part because it would clearly make them huge hypocrites: *"For if you forgive other people when they sin against you, your heavenly Father will also forgive you. But if you do not forgive others their sins, your Father will not forgive your sins"* (Matthew 6:14-15). God doesn't forgive us because we forgive. That would negate everything Jesus accomplished with His blood. Should we forgive? Absolutely, but not to *be* forgiven.

So today, my friends, know this: If you believe the Lord's Prayer is for you–and you respect it in its entirety without watering it down–*it* will throw you in a coffin, nail the lid on tight, throw dirt on top of you, then place a headstone which reads: *Here lies a Law-abiding hypocrite.* But, if you want to throw this prayer of death aside and jump off the cliff into the ocean of God's grace, Jesus will be in the water swimming with you. His grace is not *just* the most refreshing aspect of life on earth, it *is* life on earth–and life in heaven!

A prayer for you: *Dad, when I think back on the times I've recited the Lord's Prayer in locker rooms and church, I remember feeling like a robot. I now know that's not how you want to interact with us. Thank you so much for exposing the truth of the New and Old Covenants! Thank you for showing me the difference! Right now, I lift up all who are reading this, directly to you. For some, what they've just read might come as a shock, as it did for me when I first came to understand this truth. But if they, like me, want to continue to "attempt" to live by the Lord's Prayer–or any part of the Law–they must do it perfectly. Jesus said this in Matthew 5:48, James said this in James 2:10, as did Paul, in Galatians 3:10. Set them free today, in their minds. Let them know the Law is still in full force, but only for unbelievers, not us. Your Word says in 1 Timothy 1:1-14 its only use is to funnel non-Christians away from Mosaic Law-breaking and toward grace and faith in Jesus! Take us deeper into the knowledge of what He has done! Amen.*

Day 27

Who Told You That You Were Naked?

"she took of its fruit and ate, and she also gave
some to her husband who was with her, and
he ate. Then the eyes of both were opened,
and they knew that they were naked."

See Genesis 3:6,7

Shame. This is one of the lies–if not *the* greatest lie–Satan convinces God's children of. He wants us to think there's something wrong with us. From the beginning of time, this lie began. Adam and Eve were perfect in every way; physically, spiritually, and in their soul. They had the very life of God in them because of the complete absence of sin. Their life *was* God's life (see Genesis 2:7).

The enemy could easily see this fact. He knew who they were as God's own children and because he hates God, he hated them too. So he began to lie to them *about* them, just as he does to *Christians* today.

First, let's take a step back. Why would God allow Satan to be on planet earth? So that we would have the option of free will. Why do we need free will? So we would not be fleshy mannequins–so we can *choose* to love God. More importantly, so we can *choose* to believe in who we truly are as God's own creations. Once we do, we will naturally love God as well as ourselves and others. But first we must believe that we *are* loving beings.

Who were Adam and Eve? Perfection. *Love* perfected. The original prototype of God's design for us. Why were they perfect? Because they had the life of God *in* them. It wasn't because they had *done* anything at all, but because they were created as His first human children. What Adam got *wrong* as a human, Christ got *right* as a human. Jesus fixed what Adam was supposed to do, had Adam believed God about who he really was (see Romans 5).

However, from the beginning, Adam and Eve's life was a free gift *through* God's love–just like ours is *through* faith in the Cross (see John 3:16). But Satan wanted them to believe they needed more information on who they were as well as who God is. But the truth was, there was no *need* for any additional wisdom or knowledge! God and *they* were already one!

There was no reason to *know* good from evil. Yet still, the ability to choose to no longer believe this truth caused the life of God to be taken away from them–His very Spirit–and the force of sin then entered the world (see Romans 5:12, Romans 7, Genesis 4:7). So what was it that pulled their perfection away? What was it that *removed* their life, which was God's life? This: by acting on the temptation of needing to know right from wrong, according to the devil. In their spirit they already *knew* right from wrong, according to God.

The great sales pitch of Satan was:

"Did God <u>really say</u>, 'Don't eat from that tree'?" (See Genesis 3:1)

He was already pitting humans against God–our very life. He was already trying to make them doubt who they already *were*: just like their Creator in every way possible.

God had commanded Adam and Eve to not eat from that tree. Why? Was He on a power trip to "be" obeyed–as some grace-confused Christians want us to think? No. Was there anything special about that tree's fruit? No. God said, "Don't," because He knew that would be the first lie of Satan, and once they *did* choose to believe his lie, that very act would cause them to no longer believe Him about *who* they already were: complete.

He knew His very life would be removed from them, His Spirit. He cannot live inside of anything that is not holy, and if we are not holy, it is because of sin–not the verbs, but the noun. *Hamartia* is the original Greek word. And *sin* can only be inside of an unbeliever's spirit, *not* a believer's spirit (see 1 John 3:9, Romans 6:2). This is how Christ makes His home in us! This is why the New Covenant is so amazing! It is Christ reconciling us with God, through Himself, through His ability to remove sin from us by way of *simple* faith (see 2 Corinthians 5:19, 1 Corinthians 6:11, John 1:29, 1 Peter 2:24, Matthew 18:3).

God has always been interested in one main thing: *Do you believe me about who you are, and who I am?*

Adam and Eve were naked from the beginning of their life, but were never shameful. Why not? Because there was nothing wrong with them. It was when Satan sold them the bill of goods in Genesis 3, "You will be wise because you will know good from evil–and you won't die. God is lying to you. The truth is, once you have *my* wisdom, you'll be just *like* God."

After that, *then* they became ashamed, thinking, "Now I truly know right from wrong."

Friend, this continues on today in the body of Christ–His Church. We want to list off good from evil, small sin to big sin, right from wrong, wise from unwise, and lie from truth. We think we have such wisdom down to a science–to a law–yet, just like from the opening scene of time, God is still saying, "Do you believe me?"

Sadly, we will trust Christ for His forgiving blood but not for His very Spirit inside of us, to lead us. We think we need a rule book, a loud, motivating pastor–or Moses, or even Christian principles and disciplines. We think we need to be told, "This is right. This is wrong," and the evidence of what's shameful or *not* shameful can be measured by "doing" or "not doing."

The legalistic mindsets of the Jews, who were following Jesus around from town to town, wanted *Him* to tell *them* what they should and shouldn't do as well–even while He kept telling them to just *believe* Him:

"What must we do to do the works of the Father?" (John 6:28)

Do you see it? "What must we *do*?" and "What are the *works*?"

This was what Adam and Eve needed as well, according to Satan anyway. The "do" was the act of eating a piece of fruit. *Our* do can be listed off as many things, but for them, it was just reaching out, picking, and then biting. They wanted the wisdom of God *through* works...but they already had it. It was Him *in* them.

Christian, you already have it too. It's Christ in you! (See 1 Corinthians 2:16, 6:17, Colossians 1:27). For this reason, Jesus tweaked His answer after being asked that question:

"The <u>work</u> of God is this: to <u>believe</u> in the one he has sent." (John 6:29)

The work–not works–is that we believe. Believe what? Believe that by one sacrifice He has perfected us *once* again, by grace through faith, just the same as Adam and Eve were *before* they no longer believed God *about* their perfection (see Hebrews 10:10,14, Ephesians 2:8,9, 2 Corinthians 5:21).

I AM NOT TALKING ABOUT WHAT YOU DO. I AM TALKING ABOUT WHO YOU ARE. Get your *who* right and your *do* will happen naturally. Not the other way around, which is Satan's bait.

The work of God is that we believe we have all we need *in us* for life and godliness–which is the very Spirit of Jesus Christ! (2 Peter 1:3, Colossians 3:4, Romans 8:9). Not later on, but now! Not increasing over time, but right now! Yes, our unholy actions and attitudes will mature over time, but we won't. Birth is final (see John 3:6,7).

The work of God is that we believe the very same unfairness which pulled spiritual perfection *away* from mankind through the choice of Adam, is the very same unfairness that gave it *back* to mankind, by way of faith in Jesus. Through one man's disobedience we lost it. Through one man's obedience, we gained it! (See Romans 5).

Believe who you are, Christian, please. You are a saint. You are holy. You are blameless. You are full of the same qualities as the Creator of the universe! (See Colossians 1:22, Galatians 5:22,23, 1 Corinthians 13:4-8, Philippians 4:8).

"Yeah right, Matt! We gotta know what sin is and fight it!"

Friend, anything that is not of faith is sin (see Romans 14:23). Anything that is not being led by Christ, who is your life, who has perfected your spirit to *be* His life, is sin. Like Adam and Eve, we don't need "the knowledge of good and evil." Like the Jews, we don't need 613 commandments from Moses–or even what the Church has created: "Moses' Top 10 plus tithing."

We have become obedient from the heart, from identity (see Romans 6:17, 2 Corinthians 5:17). So anything that we do or don't do, think or don't think–in which we are tempted to check off as sinful–is not of faith. Instead, it's us being temporarily insane. It's an eagle who thinks it's a chicken who doesn't have the ability to fly high. It's, as Peter said, us forgetting that we *have been cleansed* from our sins (see 2 Peter 1:9).

Like Adam and Eve, we don't need the knowledge Satan offered–even if other Christians incorrectly make that their #1 goal–or label *us* as sinful because we don't do the same. Sure, there is tons of advice for godly living all throughout the pages of the New Testament. But such advice is only reiterating what's already written on our hearts. That *authentic* wise counsel comes to life through our actions and attitudes organically by *believing* who God has recreated us to be: *sinless beings who sometimes forget who we are and then incorrectly choose to sin.*

Yet grace abounds.

Sometimes this forgetfulness lasts nearly our entire human lifespan–and earthly pain is the result. Even still, our identity remains the same because Jesus will never die again, and the Father and Son will never break their promise to one another (see Hebrews 6:16-19, 7:25, 2 Timothy 2:13).

But *when* we believe God like Adam and Eve originally did, we enjoy the same Spirit in us, guiding us! His Holy Spirit will never lead us into licentiousness, debauchery, legalism, addiction, fear, angst, pressure, rage, resentment, immorality, dead works, abuse, factions, gossip, unforgiveness, racism, hate, passive-aggressiveness, dishonoring others, the silent treatment, denominations, hierarchies, or Mosaic Law. The bottom line is, *He* will never lead us into sin nor anything that will *produce* sin! So don't worry! Trust Him! He will guide us into truth moment by moment! He will guide us into the graceful knowledge of who we really are, His children!

So today, my Christian friends, let me ask you this: Who told you that you were naked? Who told you the forces of hell have any control over you? Who told you that your faith in Christ's forgiveness wasn't good enough, and that you needed to sustain it *yourself* by what you do and don't do? Who told you, like Adam, to blame someone else for *you* no longer believing God about your one-time spiritual rebirth? Who told you that you could possibly keep track of all your sins and then confess them to a man in a box to be forgiven–as if the Cross was not enough and you had to add to it? Who told you that a liquid could possibly wash away your sins? Who told you God will bless you more if you give a percentage of your money away–as if He doesn't freely give you all things because He loves you? Who told you that a pastor, church leader, or priest is more holy than you–or held to a higher standard–as if faith in the Cross *alone* is not the highest? Who told you that you *need* a human priest, as if our final Priest was not enough? Who told you that you need to exude a gift as proof you are saved–or to make God's Spirit envelop you a *second* time–as if He didn't have the ability to get it right the *first* time? Who told you that you need to go to a geographical location once a week to be good enough for God? Who told you that you are not *already* just like Christ? Who told you that you have the ability to *lose* the life of Christ in you? Who told you that God would leave you or that He is disappointed in you? Who told you that you've crossed the line and His grace is no longer enough? WHO LIED TO YOU? ... The enemy did ... You are not naked. Believer, you are fully clothed in the righteousness of Jesus Christ, forever.

A prayer for you: *Dad, thank you for teaching me what you've done for me through Jesus. What a gift. In the first conversation you had with Adam and Eve–after Satan lied to them and they acted on those lies–you asked a question in which you already knew the answer to, "Who told you that you were naked?" I believe you did this so they could see who the liar really was. The truth is, they WEREN'T naked before they believed his lies about them NOT already being EXACTLY who you created them to be. But*

their new "religious knowledge" failed them, as it still does us today. I also believe you asked them that question because you wanted them to know who it was that removed their life–your Spirit–from them, which was their own choice. I know that since we were born from sinful Adam and Eve, we inherited their sinful spiritual DNA. But by Christ, we've been reborn in our spirit! We've been given new, perfect spirits! Thank you! Right now, I lift up all who are reading this, directly to you. So many of these Christians think they're not spiritually perfect. Please help them to believe this truth! Like Adam and Eve, you clothe us when we FEEL shame, but really, we have nothing to be shameful of when it comes to our identity! Help us to believe this truth more and more each day! In our Savior's name I pray, amen.

Day 28

When Did the New Covenant Begin?

But God found fault with the people and said:
"The days are coming, declares the Lord, when
I will make a new covenant with the people
of Israel and with the people of Judah."

Hebrews 8:8

Picture it. Your brow starts to look like a strip of miniature bubble-wrap as you perspire greatly. Shocked, while staring at a huge bill you just opened up, fear begins to grip your soul. Just the same as a rock falling from a cliff, your heart drops into your stomach, "Oh my goodness...I can't afford this! What am I going to do?!"

Pacing through the house with your pulse racing and hands shaking, you glance up at the name and address on the notice–stopping dead in your tracks–"Bill and Jane Phillips? Oh thank God! Thank you, Jesus! This is not for me!"

The postman accidentally slipped your neighbors' bills into *your* mailbox! You're reading someone else's mail and this debt does not belong to you! What an amazing relief!

For us, as Christians, when we read Old Testament Scripture–the rules, regulations, and debt of the Jews *to* God–WE ARE DOING THE SAME THING. It's not our mail. Therefore, we too should feel a sense of respite once we realize such a deficit never belonged to us.

When Moses led the people group of Israel out of slavery in Egypt, they were split up into twelve tribes. The tribe of Levi was made up of priests. These priests were not allowed to have a regular job, instead, grain tithing by the other tribes was supposed to support them (see Numbers 18:26, Malachi 3:10). Many pastors today pull this verse out of context to claim we should tithe *them*, but this was for the Levitical priests *only*, and according to the Old Covenant–*and* it was so they could eat. Tithing was never meant to pay for a pastor's trip to Paris. New Covenant believers are to give freely, from the heart, not under pressure (see 2 Corinthians 9:7).

Anyway, the priests were responsible for maintaining the debts caused by Israel for *not* obeying Moses' commandments. Through their work at the temple, they were never allowed to sit down and were always presenting the blood of animals on the altar to atone for the sins of Israel–NOT CHRISTIANS. We were never invited *to* obey the commandments given to Israel, which were according to the Old Covenant. So, we never even *needed* to be forgiven *for* the commandments. On this side of the Cross, we enjoy the New Covenant of God's grace!

Was there anything wrong with the Old Covenant that planet earth needed a new one? No. It was and still *is* perfect (see Romans 7:12, 1 Timothy 1:9). The fault was found in Israel's inability to keep up their end of the bargain with our Creator:

"But God found fault <u>with the people</u> and said: "The days are coming, declares the Lord, when <u>I will make a new covenant</u> with the people of Israel <u>and with the people of Judah</u>." (Hebrews 8:8)

In that verse, the New Testament writer of Hebrews makes clear that the blame was on the people–not in the agreement. He (or she) then points out that a *new* Covenant will come from the tribe of Judah. To the Jews, the whole of Israel, this was crazy talk. "That would be impossible!" they'd retort, "A covenant can only come from the tribe of Levi because blood must be shed through a priest!"

The author of Hebrews–a former Jewish Law-follower–would have a comeback for that excuse:

"Jesus has become the guarantor of a <u>better</u> covenant."
(See Hebrews 7:22)

This New Covenant–which would come from *gasp* the tribe of Judah and not Levi–were the ancestors of Jesus! Mary came from this tribe, as did Jesus' earthly father, Joseph.

"But Matt, Joseph didn't physically create Jesus through his sperm, so how can you say Jesus came from the tribe of Judah from his side?" an inquisitive person might ask.

Oh, my friend, even *more* importantly, God chose this man to *raise* the Messiah *as* a descendant of the tribe of Judah, while temporarily here on His very own creation! New, heavenly, godly-begotten blood would bring *in* the New Covenant! (See John 3:16, Hebrews 1:1-3). At the Last Supper, Jesus explains this epiphany as He raises His cup, looking into the eyes of each disciple:

"This is <u>my blood of the covenant</u>, which is poured out for many for the forgiveness of sins." (Matthew 26:28)

God requires blood to not only forgive sins, but to bring in a Covenant. Even the first Covenant had to be sprinkled with blood *and* the people to establish it:

"When Moses had proclaimed <u>every command of the Law</u> to all the people, he took <u>the blood of calves</u>, together with water, scarlet wool and branches of hyssop, and <u>sprinkled the scroll and all the people</u>." (See Hebrews 9:19).

Gross! I'm skipping that service!

Friend, God requires *blood*–not confession, not asking, not begging, not even repenting–but B.L.O.O.D. If there's one thing you remember from this devotional, remember that God uses blood in His economy to *pay* for sins. Why do you think the hemoglobin of the Messiah was so important to the Jews? It's because they knew God wanted blood for their Mosaic transgressions.

According to the Old Covenant, the Jews felt a sense of relief each time they left the annual Day of Atonement. After handing off their best animals to be sacrificed at the temple by the priests from the tribe of Levi, they could exhale. That priest was their middle-man, their go-between, their mediator. But Christ has become the *new* Mediator! The better, final Priest!

"For there is one God, and <u>one mediator</u> also between God and men, <u>the man Christ Jesus</u>" (1 Timothy 2:5)

"For we do not have a high priest who is unable to empathize with our

weaknesses, but <u>we have one who has been tempted in every way</u>, just as
we are—<u>yet he did not sin</u>." (Hebrews 4:15)

Even the Levitical priests had to present blood for their *own* sins, their *own* messing-up-of the Law! (See Hebrews 5:3). Jesus didn't! Now, as New Covenant believers, we don't need human priests. The hierarchies are obsolete and we are one! We are *all* a royal priesthood! Peter tells the early church:

"But you are a chosen people, <u>a royal priesthood</u>, a holy nation, God's
special possession, that you may declare the praises of him who called you
out of darkness into his wonderful light." (1 Peter 2:9)

But back to the Last Supper for a moment, as they drank Jesus' new blood of the New Covenant, symbolically, *He* was being poured out into each person. Nothing magical was happening here, but instead a foretelling of Christ's Holy Spirit supernaturally entering the body of each believer. His spiritual lifeblood would now be in every human who would *ever* believe in His bloody forgiveness.

This was done not to *achieve* forgiveness, or to harp on the stuff we "still" need forgiveness *for*. Instead, the Lord's Supper is *only* for remembrance of *His* forgiveness. Today's church has turned this celebration into an emotional event of remembering *our* sins–but Jesus said, "Do this in remembrance of *me*."

Dimming the lights and evaluating our sin-management success, or lack thereof, is wrong. "I better clean up my act or I'm not worthy to drink this grape juice and eat this cracker" is poppycock!

If you think about it, when was our forgiveness available as Gentiles, non-Jews? The divider in your Bible before the book of Matthew might say *The New Testament* but that's not when it actually began. Was it when Jesus was born? Was it at the Last Supper?…No.

THE NEW COVENANT BEGAN AT THE *DEATH* OF THE MESSIAH! When Jesus' blood was shed! Just look!

"In fact, <u>the Law requires</u> that nearly everything be cleansed with blood, and <u>without the shedding of blood there is no forgiveness</u>."
(Hebrews 9:22)

What Law required blood? Moses'! The mail written to the Jews! Israel's inbox! 613 debt notices in which they could *never* pay in full, so they had to keep sacrificing their best animals to *get* annual forgiveness for sin! But this animal blood only *covered*, or *atoned for* their sins for a year. It *reminded them* of how badly they kept breaking the commandments given by Moses! (See Hebrews 10:1-4).

Yes, it paid *off* the debt, but more debt would be accumulated later that year as they continued to sin! They never confessed to a Levitical priest to be forgiven so what makes us thinks we have to? I'll tell you! Poor interpretation of Scripture! Pride! Extortion! Greed! Religion! Fear! Manipulation! Error! Their many words *never* forgave them! Instead, they handed off their cattle to the priest on the *unholy* side of the curtain *in* the temple to *be* slaughtered to *gain* atonement where *only* the Levite had access at the altar!

What a cluster of difficulty, stress, strain, and hard work to gain forgiveness of sin! Christ, however, would *take away* all of their sins–FOR GOOD! No more temple sacrifices! No more annual treks! But how?! ... By grace through faith in *Jesus'* blood, His final sacrifice (see Ephesians 2:8,9, John 3:16, Matthew 27:51, Hebrews 10:18-22).

Messiah would not atone for, or cover, but *banish* their sins into oblivion– as far as the east is from the west–which was foretold in the Psalms (see Psalm 103:12). *He* is not bound by time (see Hebrews 7:3, John 8:58), so their past, present, and even *future* sins were forgiven by God, and *chosen* to be forgotten forever.

> It is <u>impossible</u> for the blood of bulls and goats to <u>take away</u>
> <u>sins</u>. Therefore, when Christ came into the world, he said: "Sacrifice and
> offering <u>you did not desire</u>, but <u>a body you prepared for me</u>"
> (Hebrews 10:4,5)

> Then he (Jesus) said, "Here I am, I have come to do your will." He <u>sets</u>
> <u>aside the first (Covenant) to establish the second.</u>"
> (Hebrews 10:9, my notes added)

> The next day John saw Jesus coming toward him and said, "Look, the
> <u>Lamb</u> of God, who <u>takes away the sin of the world</u>! (John 1:29)

> "For I will forgive their wickedness and will <u>remember their sins no</u>
> <u>more.</u>" (Hebrews 8:12)

This wasn't even written to us, but Israel. These sins were not the type of sins the modern church normally likes to point out. Instead, they were religious sins. Sins of unbelief. The Jews were the most well-behaved people on earth. They were constantly seeking righteousness through the dangling carrot of Law observance (see Romans 3:11,20,28, Galatians 2:16). So this wasn't about repenting from skipping church, drinkin', smokin', and bar-hoppin'–but even *still*, they suffered from the worst sin of all, the unforgivable sin: *unbelief in Christ as their Messiah, rejecting His grace* (see Hebrews 10:26-29). They wanted to continue following the 613 commandments of Moses. But *we*, as New Covenant believers, get to follow the two *new* commandments of Jesus Christ:

1. Believe He's forgiven us.
2. Love as He has loved us.

These two aren't *added* to the Old's 613, becoming the New 615. The Old is now obsolete! The New is all that's available to both the Jew *and* the Gentile! (See Hebrews 8:13, Galatians 3:28). Jesus explains His new, easy commandments, in the book of John, and John explains it in 1 John:

> "*A new commandment I give to you,* that you *love one another: just as I have loved you,* you also are to love one another. By this all people will know that you are my disciples, if you have love for one another."
> (*John 13:34,35*)

> "And this is *his command*: to *believe in the name of his Son, Jesus Christ,* and to *love one another as he commanded* us." (*1 John 3:23*)

John, a Jew, said these commandments are *not* burdensome (see 1 John 5:3). The commandments from Moses *were* burdensome. The Jewish people wanted freedom from such a burden, which would only come through the Messiah prophesied about in Isaiah 53–the same freedom Jesus claimed to have access to:

> "*So if the Son sets you free, you will be free indeed.*" (*John 8:36*)

"NOPE! I'm not buying it, Matt! Jesus said we are to love God with everything we are! He said we're supposed to love Him with *all* of our heart, soul, and mind!"

Friend, I know He said this. But *when* He said this, He was just asked a Law-based question by a Moses-following, legalistic Jew. So, He gave a Law-based *answer* to a Moses-following, legalistic Jew, based on the very commandments to which that *man* was supposed to be obeying. This person was trying to trick Jesus and said, "What is the greatest commandment *in the Law?*" (See Matthew 22:36, my emphasis added).

Christ knew that every commandment was equally and *evenly* important (see Deuteronomy 4:2, Galatians 3:10). Because of this, He pulled out the commands about *them* loving God, because He knew these slimeballs were not doing anything remotely close. Loving God with "everything we are" is Old Covenant love. It's burdensome because how do we know if we're pulling it off?…We don't.

And what happens if we *don't* pull it off? Punishment? That can't be true because Jesus was already punished. Do you see it?

For years, I looked at this passage in Matthew 22 as *I gotta love God with everything I am! It's the least I can do!* But that's *not* the gospel. Anything that leaves us with the option of *us* failing God, is not the truth of the New Covenant. What is a failure according to our Creator? A sin. And what did Jesus do with our sins? HE'S TAKEN THEM ALL AWAY.

On this side of the Cross—as those who have placed our faith in Jesus—God is *counseling* us with love, not punishing us with torment or less blessings. He is *inspiring* us from within to live *out* our heavenly heritage! The gospel is this: God loves me with everything *He* is—so much so, He allowed Jesus to shed His blood to bring in the New Covenant so that *I* could receive His Spirit into my own, therefore making *me* just as righteous as Him! (See 1 Corinthians 5:17-21, 6:19, Romans 6:6-10, Colossians 3:3).

As I come to understand His love more and more—a love He has poured out *into* me, from the moment I first believed—this relational love matures and grows into me loving Him back without pressure or effort.

The truth is, His love actually *is* the Holy Spirit in us!

"And hope does not put us to shame, because God's love <u>has been poured out into our hearts</u> through the Holy Spirit, who <u>has been</u> given to us."
(Romans 5:5)

So today, my friends, know this: The New Covenant began at the Cross, when Jesus died. His willingness to take on the brunt of humanity's sin, in Himself, was a torturous thing to do. But He wasn't focused on such shame! He was focused on the joy set ahead of Him! A joy that would come to *all* who would ever believe in His forgiveness! (See Hebrews 12:2). Christ isn't dying again and again for each of our sins in heaven! He's relaxing! It's finished! The New Covenant is *here*! (See Hebrews 7:25, 10:10,12,14, John 19:30). Do you want to be a part of it? Do you want to receive the benefits of supernatural perfection today? Then simply believe Jesus has taken away *all* of your sins *once* and for all time–and He'll do just that!

A prayer for you: *Dad, thanks for Jesus. Thanks for the New Covenant. Thanks for the revelation of total forgiveness through the Blood of the Cross. Take me even further into the halls of your grace! Right now, I lift up all who are reading this, directly to you. So many of them have been taught "If Jesus said it, I gotta do it!" But that's not always true. A lot of Jesus' teachings were meant to bring hypocrites to their knees, and as believers, we've already done that. Now, we can stand tall and be confident as your kids! We can enjoy being members of your household! Teach us even more about what Christ has done FOR us and TO us, so that He can live THROUGH us! In His amazing name I pray, amen.*

Day 29

Deny Myself, Take Up My Cross, and Follow Jesus?

Then Jesus said to his disciples, "Whoever wants to be my disciple must deny themselves and take up their cross and follow me."

Matthew 16:24

Before I begin this devotional, I want to point out a fact: Matthew 16:24 *has* happened, for every believer, and it came to pass in the *spiritual* realm by faith. New Testament letters, which were written subsequently to this quote by Christ, are riddled with this truth. Here's a few explanations from Paul:

> *"I <u>have been crucified</u> with Christ and I no longer live, but Christ lives in me. The life I now live in the body, I live by faith in the Son of God, who loved me and gave himself for me." (Galatians 2:20)*

The first *I* in this verse is referring to Paul's old, sinful spirit. *It* died, and he received a new, sinless spirit, who is now combined with Jesus' Spirit. The *I* in the second sentence represents his newly created self.

He tells the Romans as well as the Corinthians, the same:

> *"For we know that <u>our old self was crucified</u> with him so that the body ruled by sin might be done away with" (See Romans 6:6)*

> *"Therefore, if anyone is <u>in Christ</u>, the new creation <u>has come</u>: The old <u>has gone</u>, the new <u>is here</u>!" (2 Corinthians 5:17)*

So let's continue, knowing that we *have been* crucified with Christ *so that* we can become one with Him as a new creation! Christian, that is what you currently are!

In the 1990's a popular phrase came out, "WWJD," which meant "What Would Jesus Do?" Most of us know this, but some of the younger people do not. It was everywhere. Merchandise flooded the market with WWJD on it–shirts, hats, bracelets–even celebrities were sporting these four letters.

"What would Jesus do?" was used in sermons and sarcasm, it sounded really neat. But doing what Jesus did is literally a death sentence *if* we are wanting to be exactly like Him in our actions. Ultimately, what *did* Jesus do? He sacrificed His perfect life for the sin of the world. We can't do that–and we aren't supposed to try. Further, God doesn't grade us on a curve *as* we try (see Matthew 5:48).

We cannot do what Jesus did. As much as those six words will upset the Type A temperament, this is reality. I understand this as true because I'm more Type A than anyone I know: *driven, competitive, sitting still isn't easy, if you're going to do something do it in the most excellent way possible no matter the time or energy it takes. Always be learning. Always be busy.*

When this personality type isn't balanced by way of the Holy Spirit's guidance, life can be miserable. We *never* find rest in our minds. But when we *are* allowing ourselves to be led by Him, He teaches us how to be well-balanced; how to enjoy not just the big accomplishments but the little things. Life is then very enjoyable and fulfilling, after we enter this rest in Him, in our *thinking*.

The enemy wants us to have thoughts that we *can* do what Jesus did. Why? Because he wants us to believe we're doing a great job at it–or a terrible job–either way, as long as we don't have rest. Denying ourselves, taking up our cross, and following Jesus is fair game to this demonic dingleberry and his crew of nitwits. Mastery or martyr, it is when we become obsessed with our "own sacrifices" we've veered off the path of grace in our thought life. Bad things happen in this ditch, and we got there because we were taught we can do what Jesus did–yet we can't. Even God isn't expecting us to.

We are branches, not the vine. Branches don't say, "What would the vine do?" nor do they *try* to be vines. They don't even try to be branches, they simply live their lives by way *of* the vine (see John 15:5).

Friend, our job as Christians is not to imitate a historical Jewish teacher. Our job is to allow His Spirit to live through us. Rather than WWJD, a better phrase would be WIJDTM–"What Is Jesus Doing Through Me?"

Truth be told, if we are to copy-cat Jesus, some bad stuff will happen because He came to straighten out *lots* of legalistic people's theology–in very harsh ways. I've never been successful at doing this. Not once.

He flipped the tables of those who were cashing in on the Law of Moses (see Matthew 21:12). He blatantly overrode everything the Jews taught (see Matthew 5:21-48). The people who believed their wonderful behavior was causing them to be right in God's eyes? Jesus destroyed them, verbally. Here's some of what He said:

"You snakes! You brood of vipers!" (See Matthew 23:33)

"You belong to your father, the devil" (See John 8:44)

"You hypocrites! You are like whitewashed tombs, which look beautiful on the outside but on the inside are full of the bones of the dead and everything unclean" (See Matthew 23:27)

"It would be better if you were never born" (See Matthew 26:24)

Keep in mind, Jesus is not chastising those who were caught in what the modern church would say is, "Nasty sinnin'!" oh no. This stuff is being shouted toward devout religious people; self-centered men and women who refused to find their identity in Christ alone. They *hated* Him for calling them out, so much so, they killed Him. Religion was more important than the very Messiah spoken about *in* their religion, who was meant to set them *free* from religion (John 5:37-40, 11:53). This continues today in churches across the world.

So are we supposed to call people snakes? Should we say they are dead on the inside, or that they should've never been born? ... No. That's what *Jesus* would have done. He's not expecting us to do the same, despite what an angry, slobbery preacher is shouting.

While Jesus was convicting religious people of their sin on *that* side of the Cross, *we* are supposed to allow His Spirit to exude His loving character on *this* side (see Galatians 5:22,23, 1 Corinthians 13:4-8). We are supposed to be ready to give an account for the hope of the gospel, expressing this truth with gentleness and respect (see 1 Peter 3:15). This takes time to learn, especially when we've been hurt by self-righteous people, but it *is* possible.

How do we pull this off? By simply being ourselves–not by *denying* ourselves, but by *being* ourselves. We are *not* supposed to do everything Jesus did–*especially* denying ourselves.

An inquisitive person might retort, "Okay, Matt. I like what you have to say here, it makes sense. But what about that verse you mentioned? The one where Jesus talks about denying ourselves, taking up our cross, and following Him?"

I love this particular Bible verse because Christ is teaching an impossible task which is always meant to bring relief. For most of my Christian life I didn't understand that anytime He taught an impossibility, Jesus was attempting to guide the listeners toward grace. Rule of thumb: if we can't do it perfectly, literally, then don't even try. Instead, believe in His ability to do it on our behalf.

Unfortunately, this passage has been used for centuries by uber-religious, behavior-focused people who believe *they* are actually doing this. They're not, and that was Jesus' whole point.

Let's lay out the Scripture in question and unfold the truth:

> Then Jesus said to his disciples, "Whoever wants to be my disciple must
> deny themselves and take up their cross and follow me."
> (Matthew 16:24)

Just like any Bible verse which is taken out of context, this too can be deceiving if we don't read around it. The grace-confused folk don't want to do this because out-of-context Scripture fits their sanctimonious lifestyle perfectly. But let's overlook that and start back up at verse 21:

> "From that time on Jesus began to explain to his disciples that he must go
> to Jerusalem and suffer many things at the hands of the elders, the chief
> priests and the teachers of the Law, and that he must be killed and on the
> third day be raised to life."

It's easy to see that Jesus is explaining the severity of what is about to happen. This is *not* a call for the disciples to do the same thing. Instead, it's meant to point out that they *can't* do this. Think about it, if they *could* do this—suffer, be killed, and raised on the third day to pay for sins—and Jesus was instructing them, "Follow me with your cross so you can be sacrificed too," then there would have been a total of 13 crucifixions. Actually, 12, because Judas wouldn't have done it. Satan was in his heart (see Luke 22:3).

Do you see it, friend? Christ is telling them what they *can't* do. They can't deny themselves, they can't take up their crosses, and they can't follow Him. So 2,000 years later He's not telling *you* to do this either. Just look at what Peter said to Him in verse 22; he had *no* interest in anyone being crucified, especially Jesus:

> Peter took him aside and began to rebuke him. "Never, Lord!" he said. "This shall never happen to you!"

Jesus followed up Peter's plea with a pretty bad burn:

> Jesus turned and said to Peter, "Get behind me, Satan! You are a stumbling block to me; you do not have in mind the concerns of God, but merely human concerns." (Matthew 16:23)

Peter wasn't Satan, obviously. But Christ knew who was influencing such a thought—the devil. This is another reason why we shouldn't do what Jesus did, that is, calling people the devil. I've tried that and did not get a favorable result.

In the next verse—when Jesus said they must deny themselves, take up their cross, and follow Him—He is explaining what it would take for *them* to do what only *He* can do. He's expressing the impossibility of anyone being able to pay off the sins of the world. Who could do such a thing? Only the Messiah, only one Cross, only one Sacrifice...only one Person denying Himself...Jesus.

He had to deny *Himself* because *He* didn't deserve to die. He was perfect in every way and only imperfect people deserve death (see Romans 6:23). This passage is not for us, but for Himself. Jesus never sinned and He knew that, so He was denying Himself of *not* having to paying for *our* sins. If Jesus Christ didn't deny Himself, none of us would have a chance to become one with God (see 2 Corinthians 5:21, Hebrews 12:2).

Therefore, on this side of the Cross–as New Covenant believers, with new, perfect hearts–*we* don't need to deny ourselves because Jesus already did this *for* us. He denied Himself so we wouldn't have to. To be clear, I'm speaking to Christians, those who have a new spirit with Christ indwelling them. You can become a Christian this very moment by believing He's forgiven you of your sins (see John 1:12, 3:16-18).

On this side of Calvary, we are not denying ourselves! We are supposed to be living life to the fullest! We are supposed to be expressing our true nature as holy people! Children of God! Saints! There is no cross to take up! It was already taken up! Everything's been finished by Christ denying *Himself* of never tasting death due to sin! (See 2 Peter 1:4, Ephesians 2:10, John 10:10, 19:30, Colossians 1:22, 2:10, Philippians 2:8).

So today, my friends, know this: If you are a believer in Jesus Christ, never deny yourself. Instead, *be* yourself! You have no cross to take up, Jesus already took it up! You are not following Jesus, either. That's what the disciples did physically and literally. You have something so much better! You are united with Him forever! (See 1 Corinthians 6:17, Colossians 3:3, Romans 6:5).

A prayer for you: *Heavenly Father, thank you for opening up my eyes to the context of Jesus' words in the gospels. For so long, I didn't understand*

that if He was teaching an impossible task it was to help us realize that only HE could complete that task FOR us–by way of faith. He set people up all the time with hopeless assignments, attempting to funnel their belief toward grace. Thank you SO much for helping me discern this! He really did come to give us rest! Right now, I lift up all who are reading this, directly to you. So many of these dear readers have been taught they need to deny themselves, take up their cross, and follow Jesus–but this was NOT instructions for Christians. We could never pay for the sins of the world by doing such a thing, only He could! We are grateful to be able to express His Spirit within us! Amen!

Day 30

What Is a Christian?

"See what great love the Father has lavished on us, that we should be called children of God! And that is what we are!"

See 1 John 3:1

If you walked a city street, a county fair, or even on the beach while asking people, "What is a Christian?" you'd get many different answers. Some would say, "A person who follows the teachings of Jesus," others would respond, "People who go to church all the time." You'd even hear, "Crazy nut-jobs."

Yet, you'd also get answers such as this: "Rude, angry, aggressive, self-righteous, judgmental, hateful, cliquey" so on and so forth. This is the saddest type of description we can receive, but this *is* what certain unbelievers have experienced from us. Mean-acting, sin-focused, religiously-devout relatives and acquaintances–those who absolutely *refuse* to be clear about what Jesus has done, are wrong.

These folks have tainted the world's opinion of us, either because they just don't understand God's grace, or they've simply never *known* God's grace, through Jesus. Instead, all they've known is religion. No *relationship*, just pressure-filled principles, spiritual "gift" expressions, rule-following comparisons, and brown-nosing a false deity they've nicknamed *God* so he'll give them stuff and not hurt them like he will those *other* nasty people. Supposed Christians who picket with signs that read, GOD HATES AMERICA, have twisted the perception of our loving God to non-believers.

Christ came to save the world not condemn the world, so we too should express this same attitude of love (see John 3:17). Not a passive-aggressive, or sweep-bad-stuff-under-the-rug garbage, but *love*. This is why Jesus said, "They will know you by your love" (see John 13:35). Not by our sin-hating, not by our condescending tone, not by our ability to confess every single sin imaginable–not *even* by our behavior repentance. But by our love.

We, whom Christ personally indwells (see 1 Corinthians 6:19), sometimes muffle Him. Does He go away? No. He's simply grieved (see Ephesians 4:30). Grieved does not mean angry, it means *grieved*. It means, "I want better for you."

Why does grieve not mean angry? Because God's anger has been satisfied in full at the Cross (see Romans 5:9). We now have peace with Him forever as Christians (see Romans 5:1, John 19:30). What could possibly make God angry at a child of His? Well, what's the *only* thing which angers God? Sin. But Jesus has taken those all away–past, present, and future–at the Cross. Future sins too? Yes. He's not bound by the time system in which He created. So now, He counsels us lovingly, no longer holding our sins against us (see 1 John 3:5, 2 Peter 3:8, John 14:26, 2 Corinthians 5:19).

Unlike the disciples who *were* following Jesus, literally, on this side of the Cross we have something so much better. We've become one *with* Jesus–His very own Spirit! We are not following Him, we are infused with Him! (See 1 Corinthians 6:17).

But we forget this amazing news quite often resulting in us *not* living out our true nature, which is the exact same nature as God's (see 2 Peter 1:4). Thankfully, He never leaves us nor forsakes us when we walk in such a fake manner. Even when we *think* we're faithless, He remains faithful because He cannot disown Himself. Christ *is* our faith, and He's enmeshed with us permanently like iron wicker (see Hebrews 12:2, 2 Timothy 2:13, 1 Corinthians 6:17).

So the answer to "What is a Christian?" ultimately comes from *you* believer. How *you* are expressing yourself represents God to the world (see 2 Corinthians 5:20). But don't feel pressured because you're not. A branch is never pressured, forced, hounded, or guilted into producing fruit. It simply lives its life connected to the vine. It is the *vine's* sustenance which produces fruit *through* the branch. Same with you, Christian (see John 15:5, Galatians 5:22,23).

Most people will never read a Bible but they *will* look to how we live. Sometimes we do a very poor job at expressing our true heavenly nature, and at other times we exude our Creator's character perfectly. However, our identity is not altered in any way, shape, or form, no matter *what* we do or don't do, say or don't say. This is what makes the gospel such good news!

The gospel is about God's commitment to *us*, not about *our* commitment to Him! Where did His commitment to us come from? The Cross! God could swear by no one greater, so He swore by Himself. The Father to the Son, and the Son to the Father. Then they sealed up that Promise with perfect blood. *This* is the hope which anchors our souls! Not anything *we've* done, but everything *they've* done! (See Hebrews 6:16-20).

You and I have become the beneficiaries to *their* promise to each *other*. By grace through faith we've inherited God's own righteousness (see Ephesians 2:8,9, 2 Corinthians 5:21). Our supernatural identity has literally changed into celestial perfection (see Hebrews 10:14, Colossians 1:22). Again, I say, *identity–not* our mindsets or conduct, but our spiritual DNA–*it* is the same as our Creator's (see John 1:12, 3:6,7, 1 John 3:1).

Therefore, we can always have confidence in the fact that our actions and attitudes will never alter what God has done to our spirit by faith. It is this truth which allows us to live out our authentic self more often than not. Why? Because we know who we actually are, *saints*. Every Christian is a saint, equally, because saint means holy. Holy means sanctified or set apart, and that is what God has done to our spirit in the supernatural realm (Romans 1:1, 8:9, Ephesians 2:6).

For me, when I don't say or do the things I know I truly *want* to say or do, I can always regroup as the Holy Spirit counsels me.

"Matthew, you are still perfectly cleansed forever. That's not changed. Here, this is how you should have responded," and off He goes, teaching me more about who I am.

Who are we? Children of God! (See 1 John 3:1). We are holy perfection wrapped up in a perfect fleshy shell! (See 1 Thessalonians 5:23). We've been born *of* God! (See 1 John 5:4). Our spirit has been birthed into the family of the Omnipotent One and we have our Dad's traits! (See 1 Corinthians 13:4-8). We *will* live out who we *think* we are! (See Proverbs 23:7, Romans 12:2). So if we think we're dirty, fear-filled, sinful worms–people who aren't worthy of Dad's love–then guess how we will express ourselves? But if we think we're loved unconditionally, protected forever from hell, forgiven in full, favored by our Father, and blessed with every spiritual blessing? What do you think our lives would look like *then*?

We can enjoy our lives *because* of this truth. Truth matters. The truth is we've been reborn in the spiritual dimension just the same as we were *once* born in the physical dimension. This is why Jesus said, "Don't be surprised at me saying you must be born again" (see John 3:7). He was talking about Nicodemus' spirit. He was talking about *my* spirit and *your* spirit. He used the example of birth because birth is unchangeable. Birth is final even when our poor choices and off-putting thoughts want us to believe it can be modified.

James said we all stumble in many ways (see James 3:2). We all mess up but *we* are not mess-ups. I never feel more like myself than when I make a mistake and then talk to God about it, "I'm sorry. Please help me with this."

But although I'm asking for guidance I *know* I'm still holy, blameless, and complete (see Colossians 1:22, 2:9,10). I have been sanctified in full– my identity–but my words and decisions are *being* sanctified over the course of my *human* lifetime (see 1 Corinthians 6:11, 15:50, Philippians 1:6, 1 John 3:2).

This isn't causing me to be reborn again and again because Christ would have to die again and again, because *only* blood forgives sins, *only* forgiveness redeems, and *only* redemption gives us new spiritual life (see Hebrews 1:3, 7:25, 9:22, Titus 2:14, Colossians 3:3,4, 1 Corinthians 6:20, Galatians 2:20).

Instead, this conversation with the Holy Spirit of Jesus Christ is leading me into learning more about who I really am as a heaven-ready person, so I can walk it out. I'm being counseled, not convicted. Conviction is only for the un-believer (see John 16:8). I'm being coached, not condemned. Condemnation is not for those in Christ (see Romans 8:1). God isn't dealing with His children on the basis of our sins, but on the substance of our perfect spirit.

I've learned to not beg Him, because I don't need to (see Matthew 6:8). I've learned to not ask for forgiveness, because I've already been forgiven in full *once* and for all time (see Hebrews 10:10). I've even learned to not stay focused on my mistakes, which would induce and inflame a debilitating sin-conscience. Instead, I simply move forward knowing that my mistakes don't define me. Jesus does (see 2 Corinthians 5:21, John 10:27).

Satan, his demons, and the power of sin want us to believe that what we do or don't do defines us. It does not. For example, the person who struggles with alcoholism, we are influenced to *believe* we are alcoholics–but we're not. What misery would it be for me to say that I *am* something sinful, but then have to deny who I really am for the next 50 years? Sounds like cruelty. Sounds demonic. It definitely doesn't sound freeing, which is what the gospel is supposed to be (see Luke 4:18).

The truth is, I am a holy saint who struggles with the tendency of getting drunk all the time, but *I* am not a drunk. I'm a heavenly spirit. I am *not* my tendencies. I am sealed up in perfection with God forever and nothing can break this seal–not even my repeated sins. The power of God's grace is much greater than the power of my sins and it always will be. The shed blood of Jesus Christ was presented for my sins in heaven *one* time. I am good with God *forever* (see Ephesians 1:13, Romans 5:20, Hebrews 1:3, 7:25, 8:5, 9:23, Colossians 2:17).

Knowing this graceful certainty is what empowered me to *turn* from this particular sin, among others (see Titus 2:11,12). I only got sober once I realized who I really was. But even if I got smashed today I'd still be just as holy because Jesus isn't dying over and over in heaven for each sin I commit, which is necessary to cause a person to become holy. He's resting just fine (see Hebrews 9:28, 10:12).

If we look at this subject even deeper, if I *was* an alcoholic, I *should* be drinking. Just the same, sinners *should* be sinning. But if I'm not an alcoholic, if I'm not a sinner, but *if* I'm a self-controlled saint, then no liquid on earth has the ability to override my hand putting a beer up to my mouth (see Galatians 5:22,23, Ephesians 5:18).

For the person who has a tendency to believe their non-stop dedication to church, mission trips, or Bible study–or "never" making a mistake–dark forces are at work in their minds too. Me, just bringing up this topic, will infuriate those who find their worth in doing this stuff. Not that anything is wrong with it, but identity can never be *found* in it–not for a Christian.

Legalism, not licentiousness, is what the Jewish race was steeped in before the New Covenant was put into place at Calvary. Before He gave His life,

Christ didn't come for the heathens. He came to set the most well-behaved people on the *planet* free, in their minds (see Galatians 4:4,5, John 8:36).

His Spirit does the same for us on this side of the Cross.

So today, my friends, know this: If you've believed Jesus has forgiven you of your sins, you are a Christian. This word, *Christian*, is a noun not a verb. *Christian* is not what we do–good, bad, or indifferent–it is who we are. What is a Christian? We are saints! We are holy people! We are free! We are new creations, spotless, and blameless! We are coheirs with Jesus Christ! We are children of the Creator of the universe! So live life, and *enjoy* your life!

A prayer for you: *Dad, thank you for giving me this life. This short trip is flying by and the older I get the faster it seems to go. You've taught me to enjoy the little things, not just the big, and I like that. I know each day is a gift from you and I'm so grateful. As your son, you've taught me many things, but I have to say that contentment might be the best lesson you've given me. Contentment in my triumphs, contentment in the mundane, even contentment in my crippling pain. You ARE my contentment and I'm thankful! Thank you for making me your child, a Christian, through Jesus! Thank you for my identity! Right now, I lift up all who are reading this, directly to you. Father, so many of them have been lied to about who you've made them to be. For the distraught believer who's been beat down verbally, unjustly condemned and shamed, let them know you've been with them the whole time. YOU never did this to them, the enemy did. People influenced BY the enemy did. Rejuvenate their soul by teaching them more about who they actually are, your cherished child. And for the unbeliever, let them know Christ wants to make His home in their spirit. First, by*

giving them a new, perfect spirit–and then by joining their spirit for good. You are knocking. You want to be invited in so you can give them life, Christ's life. You, dear reader, can become a child of God this moment. You can have a brand new Christian identity. Just believe Jesus can forgive you, and He will. If you choose this today, I'll see you in heaven, friend. Amen.

Dear friend,

Thank you so much for spending time with me through this book. I hope I was able to bring you a sense of peace and confidence in knowing more about what Christ has truly done. My prayer is for you to grow into even deeper revelations of your identity as a believer. Lastly, it would mean the world to me if you'd leave a kind review on Amazon.com, Goodreads.com, Barnes & Noble's website, or wherever you've purchased this book. Your opinion is very important and encouraging to me. I always look forward to reading reviews.

May God continue to bless you greatly, with even more knowledge, of His love for you through Jesus!

In Christ,
Matt

60 Days for Jesus, Volume 1: *Understanding Christ Better, Two Months at a Time*

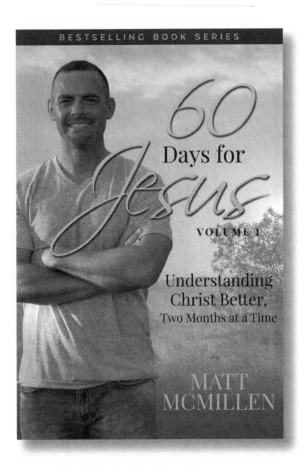

"I really like Matt's writing style. He makes understanding the gospel simple and real. I have found his daily devotions to be very helpful in guiding my walk with Christ. I highly recommend his book." -*Amazon Customer*

60 Days for Jesus, Volume 2: *Understanding Christ Better, Two Months at a Time*

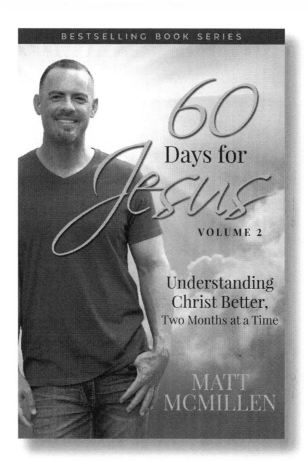

"This book is exactly what I needed to understand more about Jesus. I couldn't put it down. Thank you, Matt McMillen, for sharing your story to help strengthen others!" -*Amazon Customer*

60 Days for Jesus, Volume 3: *Understanding Christ Better, Two Months at a Time*

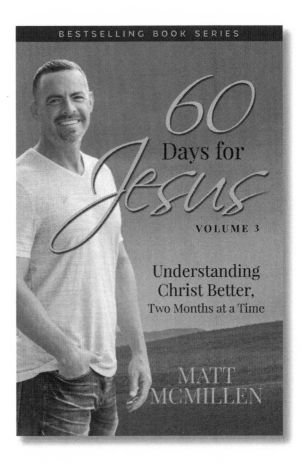

"Matt does an excellent job of providing clarity on many difficult issues every believer walks through on a daily basis. He does this by clearly articulating the scriptures to reveal the truth that really does set us free. This Volume, like the ones before, is an excellent devotional book to help any believer with their walk with God. Every page of this book is filled with the good news of God's unconditional love and grace. If you read one book this year, make it this one!" *-Amazon Customer*

True Purpose in Jesus Christ: *Finding the Relationship for Which You Were Made*

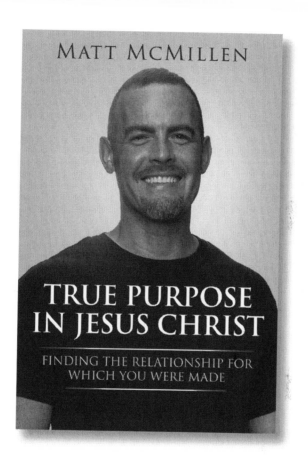

"One of the best books I've ever read! Matt's honesty about his life and what Jesus did to redeem him is amazing! He uses Scripture throughout his book to back up everything he talks about. I bought 20 books so I could share with the lost. Absolutely life changing! Thank you, Matt, for writing this book!"
-Amazon Customer

Made in the USA
Middletown, DE
28 September 2019